D0325923

DRIVEN

.

DRIVEN

TEEN PHENOMS, MAD PARENTS, SWING SCIENCE
AND THE FUTURE OF GOLF

KEVIN COOK

GOTHAM BOOKS

GOTHAM BOOKS
Published by Penguin Group (USA) Inc.
375 Hudson Street, New York, New York 10014, U.S.A.
Penguin Group (Canada), 90 Eglinton Avenue East, Suite 700, Toronto, Ontario M4P 2Y3, Canada (a division of Pearson Penguin Canada Inc.); Penguin Books Ltd, 80 Strand, London WC2R 0RL, England; Penguin Ireland, 25 St Stephen's Green, Dublin 2, Ireland (a division of Penguin Books Ltd); Penguin Group (Australia), 250 Camberwell Road, Camberwell, Victoria 3124, Australia (a division of Pearson Australia Group Pty Ltd); Penguin Books India Pvt Ltd, 11 Community Centre, Panchsheel Park, New Delhi - 110 017, India; Penguin Group (NZ), 67 Apollo Drive, Rosedale, North Shore 0632, New Zealand (a division of Pearson New Zealand Ltd); Penguin Books (South Africa) (Pty) Ltd, 24 Sturdee Avenue, Rosebank, Johannesburg 2196, South Africa

Penguin Books Ltd, Registered Offices: 80 Strand, London WC2R 0RL, England

Published by Gotham Books, a member of Penguin Group (USA) Inc.

First printing, August 2008
10 9 8 7 6 5 4 3 2 1

Gotham Books and the skyscraper logo are trademarks of Penguin Group (USA) Inc.

LIBRARY OF CONGRESS CATALOGING-IN-PUBLICATION DATA
Cook, Kevin, 1953–
    Driven: teen phenoms, mad parents, swing science and the future of golf / Kevin Cook.
        p. cm.
    ISBN 978-1-592-40394-3 (hardcover)
    1. Golf—Anecdotes.   2. Golf for children.   3. Swing (Golf)   I. Title.
    GV965.C6625 2008
    796.352—dc22   2008018299

Printed in the United States of America
Set in Janson Text
Designed by Spring Hoteling

For my mother and father

CONTENTS

INTRODUCTION

❖

BRAVE NEW GAME

Where is golf going?

That is the billion-dollar question. Golfers, golf fans and even normal people have asked me that question at PGA Tour events, country clubs and weedy public courses. There are variations: Where are all these new teen prodigies coming from? Who'll be the next Tiger Woods? Do these kids play because they love the game or because somebody's pushing them? Will they burn out at thirty?

In other words: Where is golf going?

I've been wondering, too. After twenty-five years of writing about golf, I am intrigued by the phenoms and flame-outs who are invading the ancient game. When I began writing about golfers, they swung drivers made of persimmon. The ball was a rubber-coated bundle of rubber bands. Golfers themselves were made largely of polyester and fat. For many professional golfers in the early eighties, a typical post-round workout was a set of forearm curls at the 19th hole, lifting glasses of scotch to their lips.

Not anymore. Golf is leaner, fitter, younger. Like other modern athletes, golfers now focus on fitness, diet and sports psychology. Older golfers may be playing less, but junior golf is a booming, billion-dollar business. According to the National Golf Foundation, 400,000 kids between six and eighteen years old began playing the game in 2006. Suddenly, juniors account for nearly 20 percent of America's 26 million golfers. The best of them compete in events run by the American Junior Golf Association, which began in 1978 with two tournaments. In 2006, there were seventy-five. Meanwhile the AJGA's membership has grown from a couple hundred to more than five thousand. These kids are the most talented, best-trained young athletes the sport has ever seen. They are the generation Tiger Woods inspired to take up the game— the ones he predicted would one day outplay him.

Many have advantages Tiger didn't have when he was a junior phenom fifteen years ago. Equipment, for one. Titanium-headed drivers with long, featherlight shafts help skinny teens bop drives farther than the pro golfers of twenty years ago. Balls like the low-spin Titleist Pro V1 fly farther and straighter than the balata balls of old, keeping the kids' 300-yard drives in the fairway. Fitness and modern instruction help, too. Today's teens unleash muscular, fiercely efficient swings that make Jack Nicklaus's look old-fashioned. And if they get scared on the 18th tee, their sports psychologists are there to ease their nerves with soothing words and deep-breathing exercises.

Still, something strange keeps happening. Many of these can't-miss junior superstars turn pro while still in their teens only to suffer sudden, spectacular flame-outs. They shoot to fame and then burn out in a spray of crooked drives and triple-bogeys. Why?

I spent a year looking for answers. Along the way I met some fascinating people: golf guru David Leadbetter, the sport's top instructor, teaching his swing secrets; Mu Hu, a teen hunk from Shenzhen, China, whose fans hope he'll be the Chinese Tiger; Michelle Wie, with her pushy parents half a step behind her; Gary Gilchrist, a maverick swing coach trying to steal Michelle from Leadbetter; Ivan Lendl, the stern tennis champion now playing jolly sitcom dad to three golfing daughters; shy Sean O'Hair, still haunted if no longer slapped around by his abusive father; and former phenom Ty Tryon, hacking his way through golf's wilderness.

During my year on the junior circuit, scores of players landed college scholarships, a few turned pro and at least one attempted suicide. I followed the number one junior golfer in America, Peter Uihlein, a rich, fearless kid whose father runs Titleist. I also followed the number 456 junior golfer, Michael Wade, a preacher's son who smacks 320-yard drives with used clubs bought on eBay. My time with those two and with dozens of other teens made me think that this might be the most pivotal era in the game's thousand-year history—the dawn of postmodern golf.

For many young golfers and their families, however, it is a confusing and even frightening time. If your son has talent, how should you nurture it? If your daughter might be the next Lorena Ochoa, should she turn pro at fifteen? The answers aren't obvious, but the family stories I encountered suggest that there are right ways and wrong ways to groom a golf prodigy. In fact, I came to believe that there are six essential stages in the journey from phenom to professional success. At each step, most players are left behind while a few advance.

The process starts with talent, the golfer's raw material. The next step is grit, the discipline needed to hone talent. Then come top-level teaching, financial and emotional support, a steady rise through the ranks that I call graduation, and finally a breakthrough to the game's highest level—the ultimate goal. Skipping even one step risks everything. Michelle Wie skipped a step. Tiger Woods didn't. Ty Tryon skipped step. Peter Uihlein won't.

In the end, this book is as much about families as it is about golf. It's about families driven by the idea that jumbo-size portions of love, money and desire can help their kids beat the odds in a cruelly difficult game.

This is a book about hope.

ONE

TALENT: THE FIRST INGREDIENT

David Leadbetter stepped onto the range at the Leadbetter Academy in Bradenton, Florida. The fifty-four-year-old teacher had the mottled skin and perpetual squint of a man who spends three hundred days a year outdoors in the pounding sun. More than one hundred junior golfers had gathered to listen to him. The kids sat in three rows under the range's canvas roof, which featured a giant Titleist logo. The youngest students weren't much taller than their golf bags. Few of them knew Leadbetter personally. They were trained by certified Leadbetter instructors while the guru taught lessons and made infomercials or worked with stars including Ernie Els, Trevor Immelman and Charles Howell III at tournaments all over the world. Still these kids thought of themselves as Leadbetter golfers. It was his swing they were learning. It was his name on the banner behind the range: DAVID LEADBETTER GOLF ACADEMY, THE HOME OF JUNIOR GOLF.

They sat in the shade while he stood in the sun, a craggy Ichabod Crane in wraparound shades and Panama hat. Some shielded their eyes as they watched him.

"How are you?" Leadbetter asked.

They answered together, like schoolchildren anywhere: "Goo-ood."

"I remember when we started here, ten years ago, with six or seven students. More teachers than students. We were experimenting." He shook his head as if to say *not anymore*, and got to the point. "How many of you want to make a living as a professional golfer?"

About two hundred hands went up.

"Only a few of you will make it. That's the fact. The quality of golf is getting better and better and better. To keep up, you have to be strong. Who's the best athlete in golf? Tiger!" He pronounces it *Tigah*, making Tiger sound even tougher. "Working out will be a big part of the future of the game. But you have to be mentally strong, too. Great players like Tiger have great bounce-back ability—they don't slouch their shoulders and say, 'Aww, I'm no good at this game,' or 'My coach stinks!' Great players turn their anger into birdies."

He scolded the ones who never bothered to play the Academy's own country club. "You've got to *play*. Young golfers are technically a hundred percent better than ten years ago, but do you score better, or just swing better? We've got our own course here. Use it. You can have fun on the course. Play with just three clubs—see what you can score. Hit two balls and play the *worse* ball. If you want a college scholarship, if you want a sponsor when you turn pro, you've got to learn to score low."

A final warning: "Your parents have made sacrifices so you can be here. I know some parents want it more than the kids do, but this has got to be your dream. *Your* dream."

There was scattered applause. Then the golfers stood, stretched and began hitting balls, overseen by a dozen instructors in matching khakis and golf shirts. Leadbetter paced behind them. He was "having a look"—his term for studying a swing, just as he does on PGA Tour driving ranges. To the kids he was a craggy Mount Rushmore figure walking among them; it was like going to Lincoln High School and having Honest Abe himself check your homework. A few of them got flustered, chunking shots that he politely ignored.

Carly Booth, the fourteen-year-old pride of Comrie, Scotland, wasn't flustered. She calmly thwacked perfect wedges at the sun. Carly was a born performer who liked showing off her world-class talent. Leadbetter stopped to watch her swing. He suggested a slight forward press of the legs and hips to start her swing. Lead mimed the move and Carly mimicked it, shifting her weight toward the target—"just a jot," he cautioned—before rocking smoothly into her backswing. He moved on to the next student.

A week later, Carly was still using the tip she got from the guru she called, all in one breathless breath, *Davidleadbetta*.

The David Leadbetter Golf Academy is the hub of golf's brave new world. Owned by the International Management

Group (IMG), the most powerful agency in sports, the Lead-better Academy is the crown jewel of a 300-acre Bradenton campus that features dorms, condos, restaurants, gyms, swimming pools, a private high school, a bank, a spa, a 30-acre driving range, five practice greens and, for on-course practice, the El Conquistador Golf & Country Club, which IMG bought in 2005. This junior-golf mecca grew out of the Nick Bollettieri Tennis Academy, which pioneered all-out training for kids during the tennis boom of the 1980s. When tennis faded a decade later, the golf school outgrew Bollettieri's. Golf instruction was becoming a science, with Leadbetter at the forefront. Other teachers might know the swing as well as the lanky guru in the Panama hat, but when it came to schooling young players it was Lead, pronounced "Led," who led the way.

Suppose you're the best fourteen-year-old golfer in Kansas. Off you go to Bradenton, a flat town of strip malls, car lots and parched Bermuda-grass lawns a half hour south of Tampa. You bunk in a three-bedroom on-site apartment with five other athletes. Your roomies may be golfers, Bollettieri tennis players or boys from the IMG baseball, basketball and soccer academies that share this bustling campus, where more than twelve thousand athletes come through the security gates each year. Most are part-timers, including professionals like the New York Yankees' Derek Jeter and the Boston Celtics' Kevin Garnett, who stop by during their off-seasons to use the gym's 10,000-square-foot weight room. Only about 700 junior athletes live here. Of those, 190 are golfers—hotshots from forty-three countries, teeing it up at the top golf school on earth.

Weekdays are half school, half sport. School is college

prep and lasts four hours. In that time students take the usual academic courses. The school day is short because there's no phys ed (redundant), music, shop or study hall. The golf segment of the day features three to four hours of instruction and practice, plus a sixty- to ninety-minute workout in the gym. Evenings are for studying. Weekends are for tournaments, with the occasional supervised trip to a mall, bowling alley or restaurant.

For this parents pay $70,700 a year, plus about $13,000 in private-school tuition. Academy fees include golf instruction, room and board (maid service included), gym workouts, a monthly sports-psychology session and drug and alcohol testing. They do not include tournament entry fees, clubfitting and travel expenses, which can add another $15,000, or a la carte extras like media training ($2,500) and private sessions with a sports psychologist ($150 an hour). In all, a year at the Leadbetter Academy can cost $100,000. Meanwhile, tuition and fees at Harvard add up to about $32,000 a year. But then Harvard hasn't turned out a great golfer since Bobby Jones.

Hundreds of golfers and their parents believe the Academy is worth the price. Paula Creamer, who went straight from the Leadbetter Academy to the 2005 LPGA Rookie of the Year Award, thought so. In 2006 she earned $1.3 million on the course and $4 million in endorsement deals. Some parents can quote those numbers—as well as the $20 million that Leadbetter's student Michelle Wie earned in the same year, or the $98 million Tiger Woods raked in, or even the $500,000 a little-known pro like Sean O'Hair could command just for wearing a three-inch corporate logo on his sleeve. Some parents picture a pot of gold at the end of the Academy's driving range.

But most of the moms and dads aren't like that. They are driven by something better than greed. They feel a duty to their kids' talent. One of the Academy slogans is "Don't deny your genius," and these parents buy that line on their children's behalf. Their sons and daughters dream of playing golf for a living, and the parents want to give them every chance to do it.

The term they use is "max out." Almost all of the parents who sent their kids to Bradenton in the 2006–2007 school year did it for love. They did it to help their kids reach their potential, whatever it was. They were willing to pay for the best golf training in the world even if they had to max out their credit cards to do it, even if they had to split up the family, with Dad working back home while Mom moved to Florida to be near Junior, who was dying to max out his talent as a Leadbetter golfer.

Golf talent is hard to predict. It can even be hard to describe, since it is several talents at once. A golfer needs to be a slugger who can knock the ball 250 or 300 yards on a line, as well as a finesse artist who can flip the ball up with just the right spin, then roll it over a quarter-acre green to a hole the size of a coffee can. Here is how Leadbetter describes the task: "With a hitting surface of two-and-a-half inches, you strike a ball 1.68 inches in diameter, swinging the clubhead at 100-plus miles per hour through an arc of eighteen feet. The ball is on the clubface for less than four ten-thousandths of a second and must be launched at an angle of approximately thirteen degrees. This does not take into account wind, rain or the fact that your ball is lying in a divot." Or the fact that you may be hitting puberty during your backswing.

As demanding as the game is physically, it is also "totally drive-you-nuts mental," as one junior star puts it. Every year, sports psychologist Chris Passarella asks Leadbetter Academy golfers how much of the game is mental. Every year they say it is more than 75 percent mental. "It's a different challenge than other games give you," says Passarella. "You have so much time to think." In each five-hour round, the golfer spends less than two minutes actually swinging the club. The other 298 minutes are for walking and thinking. With each step, the golfer has time to brood over the previous shot and worry about the next one, to guess and second-guess. Maybe that's why there are so many head cases in golf. Ben Hogan, the best golfer of the 1940s and early 1950s, got so nervous later in life that he would freeze over a shot, smoking a cigarette from tip to butt before he hit the ball. Half a century later Sergio Garcia, one of the most gifted young players of his time, got so mental that he couldn't hit a shot without nervously gripping and regripping his club five or six times, and sometimes ten and even twenty times. It got so bad that one day he regripped thirty-five times before he could swing.

No wonder so many junior phenoms flame out. Many of them rise from their first backyard plinks to their teens without ever losing. They rise invincibly through the junior ranks, never doubting their prowess—until they collide with other phenoms, also unbeaten but even better, and feel self-doubt for the first time. That's when the heebie-jeebies can set in.

It happens every fall at the Leadbetter Academy. Kids who were superstars in Kansas or Kyoto see their new schoolmates' swings and know that they are overmatched. This is their Academy baptism. Some quit and go home the first chance they get. Others buckle down and practice harder. Either way, everybody—everybody—loses. At least in the short term. Out of each year's two hundred or so Leadbetter Academy golfers, two or three may fight their way up to the PGA Tour or the LPGA. A hundred others will wind up scrabbling on low-rent minitours, or teaching lessons, or selling golf gear—anything to stay in the game—while another hundred wash out completely and take memories home.

On my first visit, I turned left on Bollettieri Way and showed my security pass to the stern-faced guard at the gate. My rearview mirror showed a brown weed field where tomatoes used to grow. Like much of the rest of Manatee County, the field would soon be paved and planted with condos.

I parked behind the driving range, a blanket of grass under autumn sun, and heard the *pock* of well-struck golf balls. Half a dozen instructors were teaching groups of three or four golfers each. The instructors were trim and tanned, dressed in navy or burgundy golf shirts they kept tucked into their khakis. They were all Americans or Brits. The golfers, almost all between thirteen and eighteen years old, came from the whole golfing world. One group punching wedges featured players from China, Korea, Scotland and Spain. David Whelan, who serves as the Academy's director (Leadbetter appears only on special occasions), liked the United Nations feel of this driving range. "I've learned that Scottish and American kids feel they can talk back to adults. In Korea they'd be hung," he said.

Whelan is a bull-necked former touring pro from Newcastle, England. In his playing days, his dream was to win a

European Tour event. He did it in 1988, beating a better-known Leadbetter student, Nick Faldo, in a playoff at the Barcelona Open. That was a thrill for the underdog. "Three months earlier I'd been working on the Leadbetter driving range, pouring out balls for Faldo to hit." But after his victory, the fire in Whelan's belly went out. He had reached his goal. He knew he wasn't good enough to compete with Faldo and the other Euro-tour stars week in and week out, so he quit the tour and became one of Lead's lieutenants. Now he supervises twenty-four well-trained, crisply dressed instructors at the Leadbetter Academy.

The turf around him was littered with training aids: buckets of balls, Styrofoam tubes of all colors, white-framed full-length mirrors, wooden swing-plane guides shaped like half-pipes, two-by-fours to aid alignment, sandbags to smack to build wrist strength, towels to hold under your target-side armpit to ground flying elbows. Behind Whelan were three manicured putting greens. One was ringed with bunkers for sand practice. Another was big enough to accommodate twenty kids, each one performing a slightly different putting drill. A third green was artificial turf; it drained instantly after rain.

The Bradenton Bunch, as Academy kids are called, practiced putting on the biggest green, where little white flags feature the Leadbetter logo: the guru in his shades and trademark Panama hat. There were several putting drills. In one, players stuck four tees around the hole, each tee three feet from the cup. They had to sink all four putts, then move the tees back by the length of a putter and try again. The process repeated until the tees were nine feet from the hole. Make all four nine-footers and you can yell and pump your fists like a heavyweight champ.

Another drill: Sink ten of fifteen putts from ten feet. That was quite a challenge in light of the fact that PGA Tour pros make only half of their six-footers. Yet another drill was imported from Tour practice greens: Make thirty three-footers in a row. A miss, even on putt twenty-nine, meant starting over.

For some reason science has yet to decode, boys hate putting practice more than girls. Yet no one on the Academy's greens preferred putting to full-swing practice. The kids loved to hit balls on the range. In fact, as Leadbetter had learned to his surprise, today's teen golfers would rather pound range balls than play golf. They could play for free at El Con—the players' name for the IMG Academies Golf & Country Club at El Conquistador—but preferred hitting ball after ball after ball on the range.

"We've got a beautiful facility here, better than I ever had," said Whelan, who found himself wishing he could peer inside each new arrival's heart, to see which ones were fiery like Faldo. "Some kids just live to compete. That's what you look for, and I'm not sure it's teachable."

Not that the Academy's sports psychologists didn't try. Minutes later an instructor called a youngster aside. "Eric," he told the boy, "you've got mental conditioning today."

"But I hurt my knee," Eric said.

"The knee in your head? Get going!"

Eric shouldered his golf bag, climbed onto his fat-tire bicycle and rode across a wooden bridge toward the heart of the IMG campus, a campus *The New York Times* called "the epicenter of a sports culture gone mad."

With seven hundred full-time athletes and nearly as many instructors, schoolteachers, security and maintenance workers and visiting parents, the walled and guarded IMG Academies campus is the most densely populated half-square-mile in Manatee County. Near the driving range are two baseball diamonds, their infields neatly trimmed, their chalk lines bright white. Square-shouldered boys lope after fly balls falling through a sky dotted with dragonflies. To the south and east, three manicured soccer pitches look ready for Premier League play. North of the pitches you'll find a few of the fifty-six tennis courts on campus, which include a red-clay stadium court as carefully groomed as the moms coming out of the brand-new campus spa.

The wooden bridge Eric crossed en route to his mental-conditioning session cuts through a blackwater swamp where laurel oaks, tupelo and cabbage palms grow in ankle-deep water. Beyond is one of the interlinked lagoons that connect the campus to the Gulf of Mexico a half mile away. Tall white herons and snowy egrets hunt for fish in the shallows. Now and then, a runaway tennis ball comes bouncing downhill from the courts, rolling until it splashes into the water with the birds.

Passing the pond takes you from the so-called Outback, the quieter western end of campus, where the golfers practice, to the crowded Upfront neighborhood. Up here kids swat tennis balls, scrimmage on a pair of NBA-regulation basketball courts, pump iron in a space-age gym called the Performance Institute, run sprints with parachutes trailing behind them, rush to lunch and to school and to the poolside computer lab. There are forty-eight three-bedroom dorm complexes, each with maid service and high-speed Internet. A crowded parking lot funnels cars past the barricaded front gate, where security keeps undesirables out and students in. On weekend nights, when the occasional free spirit risks expulsion by trying to sneak out, the guards use flashlights to check car trunks and backseats.

The swimming pool is the epicenter of the IMG Academies campus. Hardly anyone ever swims in the pool. There is no aquatics academy, and Academy athletes see recreational exercise as a waste of time. Why swim if no one has a stopwatch on you? For similar reasons, nobody plays pickup baseball or soccer or hoops. These highly motivated kids see no point in playing games if there are no adults keeping score.

Leathery tennis patriarch Nick Bollettieri, still spry at seventy-five, sometimes splashes a few laps, but for everyone else the pool is a meeting place, a blue magnet drawing kids to the social hub of the campus: the poolside cafeteria, where teen athletes gather at tables near a wide-screen projection TV. The usual campus-conduct rules apply in the cafeteria: no hats worn indoors, no cursing, kissing or hand-holding. The TV is for movie nights (nothing R-rated) and sports events. It is flanked by bigger-than-life photos of IMG heroes, including Leadbetter. In one corner, a venetian-blinded window guards the student bank, where athletes draw on accounts topped off by their parents.

The Academy's glossy brochures assure parents that the food here is scientifically balanced for optimal athletic performance. True enough—there are plenty of fruits, vegetables, lean meats and whole grains on the menu. But kids will be kids, and the hot-selling items are chicken nuggets, pizza, fries and cookies. A quick-serve window by the pool does a brisk business selling Starbucks coffee, the better to caffeinate late-night homework. Vending machines sell the usual chips, ice cream sandwiches and glazed Honey Buns. Yet practically no one is overweight. America's obesity epidemic is happening elsewhere. The poolside scene in Bradenton suggests that these lean, vigorous teens burn calories as fast as they burn their parents' money.

The cafeteria was the site of the first big social event of the school year. On the day of the Halloween Dance, the cafeteria window was festooned with posterboard ghosts. A sign on the door read ENTER AND DIE. As the sun sank into the Gulf of Mexico beyond the driving range, Leadbetter golfers and other IMG athletes gathered by the pool. Some chatted over Starbucks lattes. Some danced to the music leaking out of the cafeteria. Some were still in their tennis or golf togs, but as night fell there were more and more partygoers dressed for Halloween. Zombies, gangsta rappers, pirates. A boy dressed as a vampire joked that he was a sports agent.

Scottish golfer Carly Booth had chosen an exotic costume: She was a baseball player. "A very *girly* baseball player," she said of her short pants and hoop earrings. Carly wasn't crazy about the instruction she was getting in America, at least so far. A plus-3 handicap, she had been spraying the ball all over the Leadbetter range while her instructor, Malcolm Joseph, tried to perfect her swing. Back in Comrie, Scotland, her father was pulling his hair out.

"They're tweakin' me swing," Carly told her da in one of their long daily phone calls.

"*Tweakin'* it? You were brilliant before, now they've got you hitting it sideways!"

"Gotta go—there's a dance. G'night!"

Halloween was a memorable night for Carly, a fourteen-year-old girl who was thousands of miles from home as she stood on the precipice between girlhood and womanhood. Precociously shapely, with long blonde hair and gray-green eyes, she already had admirers among the boys at the party. But soon she wished she had dressed as Mia Hamm. "The soccer players are the coolest—definitely the best dancers," she said. "Some of them are from the 'hood. I saw breakdancing!"

Near the pool, a teen pirate serving as Halloween-party bouncer stopped a boy dressed in jeans and a T-shirt. "Whoa. It's a costume party," he said. "What are you supposed to be?"

"A normal kid," the boy said.

"Ha," said the pirate. "Nice one!"

ChampionsGate is a dot on the Florida map, one hundred miles northeast of Bradenton and one off-ramp south of Disney World. In the cloverleaf between the off-ramp and the interstate, developers built a gigantic faux putting green complete with a giant flagstick, as if to say, "Welcome to a totally artificial golf community." But the work done here is real.

ChampionsGate is the world headquarters of Leadbetter Enterprises. It's where Leadbetter works with Tour pros and well-heeled CEOs. Sometimes a particularly promising junior golfer makes the two-hour trip from the Academy in Bradenton to ChampionsGate for special coaching from the boss. In February 2007, Leadbetter met Mu Hu on the practice range at ChampionsGate.

The tall, craggy guru stood with his arms crossed, his face shaded by his wide-brimmed hat. His student, China's best junior golfer, sported a red polo shirt and white slacks so crisply pressed that their creases cast shadows. Mu Hu, seventeen, never wore shorts on the range or the course, preferring a PGA Tour–ready look of immaculate trousers and color-coordinated shirts, shoes and caps, even in 100-degree weather. He owned golf caps in thirty colors—but none in green. In China, cuckolded men are said to "wear the green hat."

Leadbetter watched as Mu paused for an instant at the top of his swing, completing the transition from backswing to attack. Like all expert players, Mu managed to go in two directions at once at the top of his swing. His lower body began its shift toward the target an instant before the backswing finished—part of the "swing segmentation" Leadbetter teaches. But today, while Mu's lower body shifted forward as his hands held their pose at the top, you could forget hand position, shaft angle, clubhead speed and all the other pieces of the golf swing. Forget all that for a moment and just watch Mu. Seventeen years old, handsome, lean and fit, every angle of his body in the proper relation to every other angle at the midpoint of a well-oiled Leadbetter swing: He looked perfect.

After an instant he uncoiled, the gym-built muscles of his torso twisting, pulling the clubhead through its long arc to the ball. *Bang!* Titanium clubface struck hard-plastic ball, a sound like a hammer hitting a nail. The ball leaped into the sky. It hung over the far-off treeline for a few seconds and fell to a two-hop stop 285 yards away.

"Not too good," Mu said.

"Why not?" Leadbetter asked.

"Because I suck at golf?"

"Exactly!"

They laughed. Mu pumped two more drives toward the far end of the range, both within a few degrees of dead straight. But Leadbetter had spotted a flaw. Now he had Mu start his swing in slow motion while Lead pressed downward on the shaft of his driver. "Reverse resistance," said Leadbetter. "Can you feel it?" The drill promoted what was once called muscle memory, a term that has been replaced by the more modern "NPF," short for neuromuscular proprioceptive facilitation. "NPF," said Leadbetter, "helps you feel where your body parts are as they move, so you can repeat the motion." In short, muscle memory.

"I feel it," Mu said. After Lead added resistance to four slow-mo swings, he drew back his hand and let Mu crack a drive that traced a tall, lazy arc toward the tree line.

"Better," Lead said.

But not enough better. As Mu teed up another ball, Leadbetter pulled the five-iron from Mu's golf bag. He held it so that the butt end of the five-iron's grip hovered just behind the head of Mu's driver.

"Now swing."

Mu tried, but his driver bumped the other club.

"Again," Lead said.

Another try, same result. A two-foot backswing, stopped by the five-iron.

"Again."

On the third try, Mu kept his backswing low enough to pass under the five-iron—a lower start that gave his swing a wider arc. "I do this with Ernie," Leadbetter said, meaning

Ernie Els, who also tended to lift the club a hair too soon on the way back. Leadbetter knew that an ounce of name-dropping could be worth a ton of NPF—the youngster wouldn't forget that he was working on the same swing flaw as Els, with the same teacher.

While Mu repeated the lower takeaway, Lead stepped back to watch. Reminding the boy not to drop his right shoulder, he nodded as the next ball soared into the blue.

"Mu has a beautiful swing. 'Mister One in a Billion,' we call him, but at this point he's more of a swinger than a player," Leadbetter said later. His accent, South African with a trace of his boyhood in England, made the words sound like *swinga* and *playa*. "He has all the talent in the world, but you can't just look pretty. You've got to learn to slop it around on your bad days, to find a way to get the ball in the hole, whatever it takes. That's what a *player* does."

Becoming a player entails a bit of mystery, as you'd expect in a game the Scottish writer Bruce Durie calls "a weird combination of snooker and karate." Strength helps. Size helps, too. Many of the best golfers are tall pipe-cleaner types, all angles and leverage. Still the five-foot-five Ian Woosnam, with his bleary eyes and Popeye arms, could always outdrive most of pro golf's stringbeans even after he'd had a few pints, or quarts. Teenager Tadd Fujikawa, who stands all of five foot one, routinely thumps 300-yard drives. A golfer doesn't need sprinter speed, the reflexes of a point guard or the 20-10 vision of a big-league hitter. Eye-hand coordination seems crucial, however—not only in putting but in the one golf skill that may be fundamental. For want of a scientific-sounding acronym, it's called ballstriking.

Except for the rare, mortifying whiff, every ball gets

struck. But not all strikes are equal. Some players have a knack for making clean contact. "True ballstrikers transfer energy more efficiently. All the new 3-D analysis shows it," says Leadbetter. "Shifting energy from the hips to the shoulders to the arms to the hands to the club with minimal energy loss—that's what golf is really all about."

You can hear the difference. That's why other pros often stop and look when Tiger Woods starts hitting balls on a PGA Tour practice range, even if they didn't see him arrive. They hear the percussive *pow* he puts on the ball. It's called "puring it." The difference is audible even among beginners: Listen to a group of peewee golfers and you'll hear one or two *pops* that stand out from the background noise.

Mu Hu first stood out from the crowd in China, where his father made a fortune selling and maintaining Otis elevators. In his best year, Jian Song Hu sold five hundred elevators in Shenzhen, a boomtown of 10 million people on the border between China and Hong Kong. Like a few thousand members of China's new commercial class he took up golf, and soon his 2 handicap made him one of the better players in the country. He joined Mission Hills Golf Club near Hong Kong, a luxury golfopolis featuring a dozen courses, green fees of $500 to $900, a one hundred-foot jade statue of the goddess Guan Yin, floodlights for night play and a staff of ten thousand, including three thousand caddies.

"I was OK in golf," says Jian Song Hu. "Mu, better."

And taller. "I was huge. Five-ten at eleven years old," says Mu. Six years later he is still five foot ten. His English is now perfect, without the *like*s and *y'know*s American teens use, though he still thinks in Mandarin, or occasionally in a blend of the two languages—Manglish. At eleven he won China's Junior Golf Open, beating the country's best seventeen- and eighteen-year-olds. An only child (Chinese law generally allows a family only one), he was the focus of his parents' love. They bought him the best clothes and equipment. They flew him to tournaments around the country, and that summer a Leadbetter assistant stationed at Mission Hills spotted Mu. Or rather he heard Mu, who pured his metal driver with a ringtone the instructor never forgot. The next thing Mu knew, his mother and father sat him down and said, in Mandarin, "We are moving to Florida so you can work with David Leadbetter."

Eleven-year-old Mu wanted to cry. He had never been to America. The only English words he knew were golf terms: birdie, bogey, Titleist, Tiger. Remembering his duty to his mother and father, he bit his lip, and that fall the three of them flew from Hong Kong to Newark to Tampa, and then drove south across the Sunshine Skyway Bridge to Bradenton. Mu recalls the blue of Tampa Bay, white Florida sun and road signs in a language that looked like hieroglyphics.

To the degree that a Chinese teenager who owns more than fifty golf outfits and drives a $60,000 BMW to school can be called typical, Mu Hu is a typical modern golf phenom. He is an only child from an affluent family. He took up the game at an early age, before the third grade, and started dominating his peers before he turned twelve. He was tall for his age. He competed with his father, surpassed his father and graduated to tournament play against older kids. And his hero was a California junior golfer who had performed a miracle: He made golf cool.

Modern junior golf began on October 6, 1978. That was the day Eldrick "Tiger" Woods toddled onto TV's *Mike Douglas Show*. Tiger was 980 days old. The top of his orange cap barely reached the level of his father's belt. Standing on an Astroturf mat, two-and-a-half-year-old Tiger hauled his little driver back until the shaft paralleled the floor. His ankles and knees shifted forward as the club paused for an instant—the transition Mu Hu would master almost thirty years later. Then, *pop*, he belted a ball into the blue backdrop of Douglas's soundstage.

Eldrick "Tiger" Woods was the only child of retired army officer Earl Woods and his second wife, Kultida, a Thai woman Earl, a Green Beret, had met during a tour of duty in Vietnam. They nicknamed their son Tiger after a South Vietnamese soldier who had saved Earl's life in combat. Long before he could walk, Tiger would sit in a high chair in the Woods' garage in Cypress, California, watching his father hit golf balls into a net. Those practice sessions are often credited with spurring Tiger's love of golf. Recent work in neuroscience suggests they may also have had a direct role in shaping his talent: Researchers have shown that a group of brain cells called mirror neurons fires at two different times— when a person performs a movement, and when he sees someone else perform a movement. It's as if watching were a form of internal practice. Mirror neurons may explain why Tiger developed a sound swing so quickly. By the time he was old enough to hit a ball, he had watched Earl hit thousands. (The purest example of all may be Phil Mickelson. A natural right-hander who began imitating his father at the age of eighteen months, Mickelson literally mirrored his dad's swing—by swinging lefty.)

Earl Woods signed his son up for lessons when Tiger was four. From then on, the boy made dozens of technically sound swings in a typical practice session, thousands in a month— perhaps a quarter of a million swings by the time he turned twelve, each swing reinforcing muscle memory, amplifying the move he had mirrored in his father's garage. Tiger specialized in golf so early in life that he never became a quarterback or Little League star. He wasn't cool in school. In fact his college friends at Stanford, appalled by his clumsy moves on the dance floor, would call him "Urkel" after the goofy, lovable nerd on *Family Matters*. But no one else transferred energy from golf swing to ball the way Tiger did, and no one had a better head for the game. In fact Tiger's mind was as carefully nurtured as his swing. His mother, Tida (short for Kultida) honored her Thai heritage by taking the boy to meditate in a Buddhist temple in California when he was growing up—the perfect training for golf's combination of Zen and violence. It was Tida who told her son how to deal with his junior-golf opponents: "Step on their throats."

Tiger's parents knew that nurturing a prodigy was a tough assignment. There was no training manual. But they embraced the task with what Earl called "total commitment." Earl's drive to turn Tiger into the world's best golfer damaged his marriage, as he later admitted. His bank balance dwindled. His three children from his first marriage didn't appreciate it when he called them a "trial run" for training Tiger. Still Earl Woods stuck to his mission.

A key part of the mission was bringing Tiger along *slowly*. Earl swore his son would compete only with kids his own age, no matter how badly he beat them. He wanted Tiger to win at every level, not jump ahead and start losing and doubting himself. But in 1987, Tiger put his dad's go-slow plan to an early test.

At that point the eleven-year-old phenom stood five foot one, weighed eighty-four pounds and had just started driving the ball two hundred yards. Earl knew his son could beat fourteen- and fifteen- and even eighteen-year-olds, but he kept telling Tiger those older kids could wait. "There's no hurry," he said. That year he entered Tiger in a full slate of twelve-and-under events—thirty-six local and national tournaments, most of them with fields of at least a hundred golfers. Tiger won them all.

For years, people asked: Are golfers athletes? But that old debate had it backward. The question should have been, Are athletes golfers?

They weren't. Until recently, golf was for country-club kids and their out-of-shape elders. Even in that doughy population, the best athletes played tennis. Then came Woods, creating a dashing, muscled-up brand of the staid old game. His popularity brought millions of new fans and new wealth to the game. In 1995, the year before Woods turned pro, the PGA Tour's total purse was $63 million. Ten years later it was $250 million. Two decades after Curtis Strange led the Tour's money list with $542,000, Tiger tipped his caddie more than that.

The Tiger Effect led a generation of young athletes to pick up the game, with visions of trophies and Nike ads dancing in their heads. Perhaps the most talented of them all was a giggly preteen from Hawaii.

In 2001, Blaik Shew was trudging between saguaro cacti on a toasty morning in Phoenix. Shew, a workaholic who was one of Leadbetter's trusted lieutenants, had been following a Leadbetter golfer in a women's tournament. His eyes popped when another player smoked a 270-yard drive.

Shew saw a woman applauding the drive. "Is that your daughter?" he asked. "How old is she?"

"Eleven," said Bo Wie.

"No, I don't mean how long she's been playing—"

"She's eleven years old."

At that moment Leadbetter was on the range in Orlando, having a look at another player. His cell phone squirmed in his pocket.

"David, I just saw the greatest player in women's golf history," Shew told him. "She's eleven years old."

"I'll believe that when I see it," said Lead.

Soon he would see and believe.

Michelle Wie grew up in Honolulu, where her father, B.J., was a professor of transportation at the University of Hawaii. She began hitting balls before she reached kindergarten. Tennis balls. "She was a tennis kid, and that shaped her worldview," a friend says. "At eight, nine, ten years old, Michelle was so much better at tennis than all the other girls that her dad said, 'You should play against the boys.' And she did. And she beat them, too, and that impressed her dad. Naturally she thought that the way a girl really proves herself is by beating the boys." Soon Michelle took up golf, her dad's favorite sport.

Already five foot nine at age eleven, she was the big little girl on Oahu's public courses, the girl with the purse full of five-dollar bills—money she'd won betting with her dad's golf buddies. When she turned twelve, her parents signed her up for a Honolulu clinic given by Gary Gilchrist, who was then running the Leadbetter Academy in Bradenton. Gilchrist remembers standing on the range in Hawaii, watching a few dozen kids slap the usual assortment of grounders and pop-ups. Except for a lanky, sable-haired girl who was calmly puring drives over a chain-link fence 250 yards away.

"When you see talent like that, it's like falling in love," says Gilchrist, who grew up in South Africa, playing junior golf with Ernie Els. Gilchrist thought this willowy Hawaiian girl hit the ball as well as Els had at the same age. He thought Michelle might be a history maker—the best female athlete any sport had ever seen. He convinced B.J. and Bo Wie to fly their daughter to Florida.

"There was nothing very wrong with her swing," says Leadbetter, who credits Hawaii's fine junior-golf program with keeping Michelle on the right track. Had she been born almost anywhere else, her swing might have been ruined before he ever saw her. "What was really striking, though, was what a remarkable physical specimen she was—a very young girl who was bigger, stronger and longer off the tee than some of the men on the PGA Tour! Watching Michelle hit the ball, you felt you were seeing women's golf skip a generation."

By 2003, B.J. and Bo Wie were in a tricky position. Their daughter was the best thirteen-year-old golfer in the world, male or female. "I mean, she was better at that age than anyone had *ever* been," Leadbetter says, "and then she improved. Michelle and her parents had some choices to make."

Michelle Wie might have become a famous tennis player. She chose golf instead. The same was true of a Leadbetter golfer whose father *was* a famous tennis player.

For 270 weeks from 1983 to 1990, Ivan Lendl was the number-one tennis player in the world. Dark and unsmiling, he was billed on the cover of *Sports Illustrated* as "The Champion Nobody Cares About." Lendl was a socialist-realist poster come to life, a man of lean muscle and iron will. Few athletes ever worked harder than the man *Tennis* magazine called "the game's greatest overachiever," but compared to the colorful Americans Jimmy Connors and John McEnroe he seemed like a robot. McEnroe shouted and emoted. Connors celebrated victories by clutching his crotch and shaking it at the world. Lendl just gritted his teeth and beat them both more than they beat him. Between 1981 and 1991 he made nineteen Grand Slam finals and won eight major titles, including three U.S. Opens and three French Opens.

And it turned out that the robot had a secret. Behind Lendl's iron mask was a funny, self-deprecating golfer you'd love to have in your foursome.

In his tennis days he'd had two coaches, both of whom had only daughters, no sons. "I teased them mercilessly," Lendl recalls. *Are you real men?* he'd ask. *Do you lack something between the legs—testosterone?* Then Lendl and his wife, Samantha, began having children of their own. "Daughter, daughter, daughter, daughter, daughter," he says. "Five girls. They've got me surrounded!"

Today, Ivan Lendl walks fairways at junior golf tournaments, carrying a folding chair he unfolds at strategic viewing points where he can rest his bones and watch his girls' approach shots. At forty-seven he is heavier and ruddier than in his playing days, with a salt-and-pepper buzz cut. He moves slowly, pained by the balky spine that ended his tennis career in 1994. Asked how much tennis he plays these days, he smiles. "Exactly as much as I want," he says. "None!"

In 2007, Lendl's daughters ranged in age from nine to seventeen. Marika, the oldest, had played tennis until injuries dogged her out of the sport. Switching to golf kept her healthy and got her more time with her dad, a scratch golfer who once played nine holes on the eve of a U.S. Open tennis semifinal, then went out and won the next day. Next came twins Caroline and Isabelle: Caroline rode horses and hoped to be an Olympian. Isabelle, tall and blonde, had a chance to be the next Annika Sorenstam.

At fifteen, Isabelle Lendl had her father's long face and razor cheekbones, plus the regal gait of a girl who knows she is special. "She used to slouch," Ivan says, "but I told her, 'Stop it. The way you move sends a message.'" He taught his daughter to walk with her head up, eyes up, taking in every bit of information from the slope of the green to the wind to the other players' moods. Now Isabelle looks as determined on the course as Ivan used to look on the court.

Another daughter, Daniela, thirteen, already ranked in the top 300 junior-girl golfers in America, while nine-year-old Nikki was just starting at the Academy. Both swore they'd beat their big sisters someday, and if you asked hard-nosed Daniela, whose nickname was Crash, she'd say that day might be tomorrow.

When the older girls were toddlers, they would race up the stairs of the Lendls' ten-bedroom mansion in Goshen,

Connecticut. Marika, the biggest, shoved her sisters back so she could win. Samantha Lendl wanted to stop her daughter, but Dad said no. "Let them go. This is how they learn to compete," Ivan said.

Later, Marika and Isabelle played a card-matching memory game for fun. Ivan thought that was crazy. Why play for nothing? He turned the game into a little casino: The girls played for M&Ms. Marika cleaned up, Samantha remembers. "But after two months Isabelle caught up and won back her M&Ms."

Marika was one of the American Junior Golf Association's top ten female players in 2006, but her little sister was a little better. By the end of the year Isabelle would rank second in the nation. She didn't hit the ball as far as Marika—not yet—but had a knack for hitting the right shot at the right moment. When the chips were down, you'd put a dollar chip on Marika and a five-dollar chip on Isabelle.

In February 2007, Ivan followed Isabelle around the Harbour Town Golf Links in Hilton Head, South Carolina. She was chasing the lead in the Verizon Junior Heritage, an important early-season tournament. Isabelle was the defending champion. The air was so cold you could see puffs of breath from the usual junior-golf galleries—a handful of parents and a college golf coach or two. Lendl came prepared for chilly weather. "Check it out," he said. "I have a wool hat, long underwear, rainpants and rainsuit. Golf is preparation!" The Adidas stocking cap he got for free, comped by his longtime sponsor. But he had paid for the rest of his cold-weather gear, plus the folding chair: "Twelve bucks at K-Mart," he said proudly.

Isabelle had won the previous year's Junior Heritage as a

fourteen-year-old, beating world-ranked girls two and three years older. Now, at fifteen, she was expected to win again. But she struggled that day, hitting iron shots to the greens' fringes instead of near the flags, making pars and the occasional bogey. She was nervous. This was her first time as defending champion at an important event, and she was afraid she'd fall apart under the pressure of being expected to win. Her father had said there was no pressure. "Do you know what it means to be defending champion?" he'd asked his daughter as she chewed her nails. "It means you play well on this course, that's all. Now go play it."

His advice didn't help. Isabelle didn't want the burden of defending her 2006 title, at least not today. She wanted to blend in with the other girls. She wanted to take the easy way to the parking lot.

"Look at her," Ivan said as his daughter climbed a rise toward one of Harbour Town's small, tricky greens. "She's talking to the other girls, 'Yap yap yap,' when she ought to be on the green, reading her putt. That will go in my report." After each round, Ivan sent a text message to Isabelle's swing coach at the Leadbetter Academy. Mental lapses like Isabelle's yap-yap-yapping bugged her father more than bad shots.

On the final hole of her first round, she needed a birdie to save a mediocre day. "This is a good test," Ivan whispered. "Let's see how she does."

Junior golfers usually carry their own golf bags. On the 18th at Hilton Head, Isabelle dropped her bag, pulled out her eight-iron and stared at the flag 135 yards away, uphill, ten paces from the spot where her eagle-eyed dad sat in his folding chair beside the green. They both knew that this shot had a certain existential heft. It could determine whether the first round of her title defense was a good day or a missed chance.

Isabelle swung. A spray of turf at impact, the ball shooting straight at the flag. A one-degree error at impact can spoil an approach shot—one degree is the difference between a tap-in birdie and a six-foot putt. But there was no error this time. As Ivan Lendl leaned forward, craning to follow the arc of the ball, Isabelle's eight-iron bit the green and scared the hole. It stopped six inches from the cup.

"Good girl," he said under his breath.

A few minutes later, father and daughter walked off the course together.

Mu Hu was at Hilton Head, too. On the night before the Verizon Junior Heritage, he queued up with the other players—a single-file row of thin, fresh-faced teens in spotless golf togs—to collect the free goodies the tournament's sponsor provided. Each golfer's parents had paid a $250 entry fee. Each golfer got a dozen Nike One balls, a pair of golf shoes, a glove and a Verizon phone card that was good for international calls. The card was a boon to the foreign-born players. One junior girl said, "Good deal, I'm calling *mi madre.*"

"I'm calling my boyfriend," another girl said.

The next morning they loosened up on the driving range, then moved to the practice putting green a few minutes before their tee times—the same routine touring pros follow. The boys played from the black tees, the girls from the whites. That made course designer Pete Dye's tight, tricky Harbour Town links play at 6,805 yards for the boys, only 168 less than the pros faced in the PGA Tour's annual Heritage Classic. The girls' yardage was a more forgiving 6,010. As in other junior events, the difference suited a teen game in which 250 yards is a big drive for the girls but a mediocre one for the boys, who need to sock the ball 270 to 280 if they don't want their buddies to suggest they move up to the girls' tees.

Galleries were sparse. At junior tournaments you can hear the players mumble to themselves when they miss putts. The best might be followed by a couple of college coaches wearing school-logo baseball caps to advertise their presence. The coaches scout junior golfers and curry favor with the stars, who are flattered when a big-time head coach like John Fields of the University of Texas takes time to watch them. At Harbour Town, Fields watched Mu three-putt to make a double bogey. He knew Mu's story: Chinese phenom who looked like a world-beater at age eleven, just as Tiger did, only to struggle as he tried to take the next step. "He's erratic," said Fields, "but you've got to like the way he contacts the ball. It sounds good. He's got a lot of upside." Another college coach loved Mu's swing but wouldn't recruit him for fear of losing him to the pros in a year or two. College golfers who turn pro before they graduate can cost their schools scholarships.

Mu's father had flown from Hong Kong to Orlando to join his wife and son for the six-hour drive from Champions-Gate to Hilton Head. He commuted several times a year from Shenzhen, going from a first-class seat to a chairbrella—

a hybrid gadget with a folding umbrella at the top, a spear tip at the bottom and a plastic seat in the middle. Golf parents poke their chairbrellas into the ground, deploy the seat and perch (unsteadily, like pole sitters), watching the action. Many parents get more nervous than their children. Jian Song Hu, rolling his eyes after Mu lipped out a four-footer, looked stricken.

"Three putts again!"

Mu studied the hard blue sky. A stretch of three rotten holes, featuring a drive that hopped sideways out-of-bounds and a pair of three-putt greens, had ruined his week in the course of half an hour. He was tired. Tired of messing up. Tired of thinking. He had been working on a school paper during the long drive from Orlando, a fourteen-page report about steroids, which he doubted could help golfers. "Steroids won't make you a better putter," he said, "or a better thinker." The paper was due on Monday morning; he would finish it on the drive home after Sunday's disappointing final round, tapping on his laptop in the dark, in the backseat of the family Lexus SUV.

"Steroids won't motivate you."

You have to do that yourself.

Tiger Woods, Mu Hu, Michelle Wie, Isabelle Lendl and thousands of others started out with world-class talent. They could all transfer energy to a 1.62-ounce golf ball more efficiently than 99.99 percent of the world's 60 million players. But talent is only the first step.

"In tennis, a prodigy might have so much pure talent

that you *know* he's gonna win Wimbledon someday," says Leadbetter. "Golf is different. Golf is trickier. Talent plays a huge role, of course, but so does something else, something that's harder to define." Something as hard and precious as a pearl.

T W O

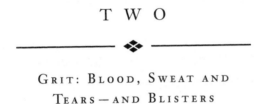

GRIT: BLOOD, SWEAT AND TEARS — AND BLISTERS

Leadbetter sat in his office, resting his chin on a long, bony hand. He kept the lights dim to give his sun-drenched eyes a rest. "The game is changing," he said. "Kids are focusing exclusively on golf at the age of six or seven. Some have no talent, but others have enough to imagine they're gonna be the next Tiger Woods. Sometimes it's the parents who do the imagining, but it's the kid who's got to do the work, years and years of practice. We're not used to seeing this sort of work ethic in children, but we're seeing it now. Our kids would rather practice than play."

He wasn't kidding. Academy golfers could play at the IMG-owned country club for free, but few bothered. Ambitious juniors from seven to seventeen pounded range balls instead. The Academy's practice facility wasn't lighted, but not to save energy—the lack of lights kept kids from pounding balls after dark. Golfers' parents sometimes beat the rule by parking behind the range with their lights on, so their backlit kids could hit balls into the dark.

This sort of work ethic had the logic of an arms race. Young players often said that if they weren't practicing, they knew some other kid was. The same sort of thinking drove parents to the Leadbetter Academy and other boarding schools that were springing up in imitation of it.

"Before long, many if not most professionals will come out of modern training programs," Leadbetter said. "We'll still get a free-range golfer out of the boonies from time to time, but most of the best players will be, shall we say, factory-produced."

It seemed a weird fate for a muddy old game that began with shepherds knocking rocks around Macbeth's turf. But the guru didn't see it that way. He saw scientific training as the next step in golf's evolution. It could even make wishes come true.

"Kids dream of making a living in golf," he said. "And if you have a dream, isn't it good to give it a chance?"

The golfers wake at dawn. They eat healthy breakfasts—granola, bananas, skim milk—and throw their lightweight golf bags over their shoulders and grab their beach cruiser bikes and ride to the gym to join other young athletes yawning and loosening up at 6:45 a.m. The gym is a vast, hangar-like building called the International Performance Institute

(IPI), with a 10,000-square-foot weight room. Inside, burly professional trainers run the youngsters through sixty-minute workouts. After forty-five minutes the golfers take a break to gulp down smoothies made of whey powder and Gatorade. The smoothies range in color from blue-brown to orange-brown.

After the workout comes a half day of school. Most Academy golfers attend the on-campus Pendleton School, the least demanding of three private schools they can choose. Owned by IMG, the Pendleton School turns a profit every year. A low-slung rectangle with aluminum-siding trim and flower boxes at the windows, the K-through-12 school is virtually paper-free. Laptops are mandatory; homework gets done online—often from a hotel room or clubhouse at a junior-golf event. Pendleton officials don't mind admitting that sports are at least as important as schoolwork: "Athletics and academics are on par," says headmaster Rich O'Dell. One hallway poster at Pendleton shows Great Americans George Washington, Michael Jordan and John Elway. A report posted outside a Spanish classroom reads, *Tigre Woods es un famoso atleta, pero el son tambien una persona buena.* Yet for all its emphasis on sweat, Pendleton doesn't drag its knuckles academically. With three shifts of highly paid teachers and only eight to twelve students per class—less than half the typical class size—Pendleton outperforms other Florida high schools despite the fact that many of its students speak little or no English when they arrive. The typical, highly motivated Pendleton student scores 1,040 on his SATs, versus 993 for the average Floridian. According to college-placement advisor Anne-Marie Vandermerwe, 94 percent of the class of

2006 went on to college. Almost two dozen seniors received golf scholarships to NCAA schools. 4 percent of graduating seniors put off college temporarily, while 2 percent went straight to the pros. "None of them went to real *work*," she says.

"These are great kids—motivated achievers," says headmaster O'Dell. "They're going to be leaders."

Pendleton's sports teams strike fear into opponents' hearts. Playing local Christian academies and other private schools, the Pendleton Panthers basketball and baseball teams trounce opponents while taking pains not to run up the score. In a hoops game early in 2007, the basketball Panthers led 21–4 before letting the third string finish off a thirty-two-point victory.

There is no Pendleton golf team. It wouldn't be fair. "We don't need to win high school golf championships," an IMG official says. "Why piss off the whole state of Florida?" That policy leaves the way clear for another local school called the Bradenton Academy, which a handful of Leadbetter golfers attend. In 2000, the Bradenton Academy golf team, led by Ty Tryon, won the state championship by twenty-nine strokes without a single team practice. The year before that, the Bradenton Academy girls' team, starring a pair of Leadbetter preteens, won the state title by a record eighty-two strokes.

After lunch each day, the Leadbetter golfers report to the range for three to four hours of practice. Some follow an alternate schedule—practice in the morning, school in the afternoon—but they all work out and hit thousands of balls a week. On weekends they play tournaments and hit more practice balls. They all work harder at their sport than pro golfers used to work before Tiger Woods remade the game in his own unyielding image.

Thursdays are club-fitting days for the Leadbetter kids. The genial, sunburnt Larry Jones camcords golfers' swings, reads numbers off his launch monitor and then re-grips and retools players according to variables including clubhead speed, launch angle, spin rate, shaft length, lie and loft. Jones matches player to weapon, then bills the golfer's parents for the clubs he prescribes, which cost from a few hundred dollars to a few thousand. The kids strike clean white Titleists on the lush, 30-acre Leadbetter range. There are no bad swings, just the rhythmic motions of supple youngsters with the powerful upright swing Leadbetter teaches. There are no screens along the sides of the range, either—these kids hit the ball straight. Or *almost* straight. As Jack Nicklaus always said, a perfectly straight golf shot is an accident. Even a low-spin modern ball revolves fifty times per second, making it curve in flight, and so the ideal flight path is a controlled draw or fade. The preference in Bradenton is a high draw. With good reason: The ball may remain on the clubface for only .00035 of a second, but in a perfect swing the clubface is starting to close in that split second, imparting a breath of right-to-left spin. Thus ball after ball on the Leadbetter range tails slightly to the left as it climbs and falls.

Charlie Winegardner, seventeen, likes hitting driver. He pounds balls that carry 270 into the wind, drawing about five yards on their way to the far end of the range. Charlie played high school basketball back home in Lothian, Maryland, but left his hometown, teammates, friends, parents and a bedroom full of trophies behind "to see if I can max out my golf."

He got off on the wrong foot the week he arrived, or rather the wrong hand: He holds the club with a baseball grip, which his instructor says will never work. Charlie says he won't change. This is the grip his dad taught him; it feels right.

Arnond "Bank" Vongvanij, seventeen, launches drives a mile high. Small, compact Bank comes from Hawaii, where his Thai mother, who was studying finance, took an exam the night before he was born. "She aced it, too," he says with pride. "So she called me Bank. She always thought I'd be a banker." Now he hopes to bank some of those giant cardboard checks that go to PGA Tour winners. Why does Bank hit so many drives that graze cloud banks? "Because when the wind's behind me," he says, quoting a Nike commercial, "ball go far."

Carly Booth's father built a golf course on his farm in Comrie, Scotland. It wasn't enough to keep her home. Today, Scotland's best young golfers go to Florida to learn the auld game. "I looove the weather," says fourteen-year-old Carly, rolling the vowel. "It's sunny constantly!" But she might not be cut out for Academy life. Blonde and flirty, she distracts boys and vice versa—a potential problem on a campus where the rules forbid public kissing and hand-holding. Carly also likes to eat, sleep in now and then and skip the odd workout in the gym. "She has some talent, sure," says one instructor with a shrug. "But how hard will she work?"

Tall, cocky Peter Uihlein (pronounced YOU-line) is all waggle and swagger. He's got a short backswing and a rapid coil-and-uncoil that whips the ball on its way. His Titleist shirt, cap and clubs come from his father, Wally, the chairman and CEO of Acushnet, Titleist's parent company. "I can't escape my dad's shadow, so why try?" says Peter, seventeen, standing in the shade of the Titleist-logoed banner that shadows the range. The most versatile golfer at the Academy, Peter can smash the ball high or punch it low. He can spin it or flop it spinlessly out of heavy rough. He can also name the three youngest players ever to win the AJGA's Player of the Year award: Tiger Woods, Phil Mickelson and Peter Uihlein.

Each of these teens has already struck more golf shots than serious players used to hit in a lifetime. By one estimate, the average Leadbetter Academy golfer has hit more than 250,000 range balls by the time he or she graduates; has played more than two hundred tournament rounds and written a report on every one; has worked out in the gym for one thousand hours and spent five hundred hours—three solid 24/7 weeks—simply reading putts.

Trainers at the IPI gym have a line about the Leadbetter golfers: They can drive a ball a mile, but couldn't catch one if you lobbed it from two feet away. The golfers of the Academy are klutzes in everything but golf. The line is an exaggeration, but there's no doubt that golfers are specializing earlier than ever before. So are kids in other sports. Neuroscience has something to say about that, too: It might not be a bad idea.

Repeated motion spurs the body to produce myelin, a fat that insulates nerve fibers. More repetition puts more myelin around the neural pathways associated with that motion, allowing nerve signals to move more smoothly and quickly. It's like greasing the skids, turning nerve pathways into superconductors, and it works best in the young. This process helps even more if you're performing a series of moves that involve many muscles. An error of four milliseconds, the time it takes a fly to flap its wings, can throw off a golf swing with its many coordinated motions. That's why it is vital for young golfers to get proper instruction early in life, before bad habits mess up the wiring. "What do good athletes do when they train? They send precise impulses along wires that give the signal to myelinate that wire," the neurologist George Bartzokis told *The New York Times*. "They end up, after all the training, with a super-duper wire—lots of bandwidth, highspeed T-1 line." Super-duper wire that makes the right moves automatic: Muscle memory strikes again.

There's no shortage of myelin in action at the Leadbetter range. Almost all the Academy's top players took up the sport when they were ten or younger and got solid instruction from the start. Almost all had gone on to hit thousands upon thousands of balls here in Bradenton, where their instructors taught the repeatable, endlessly drillable Leadbetter swing. Yet only one in a hundred would ever reach the PGA or LPGA tour. Those few probably had more myelin than the rest, but they also had more grit.

In twenty-first-century golf, grit means something more than the gumption of boyish amateur Francis Ouimet at the 1913 U.S. Open, beating England's hero Harry Vardon, or the guts of Texas hustler Lee Trevino, betting money he didn't have. It is more like the grim drive of Ben Hogan, digging wisdom out of driving-range dirt. It is a willingness to spend hours, weeks, months, *years* honing your swing until you can max out your ballstriking talent with almost every strike. A willingness or better yet a *desire* to beat balls while other kids hang out at malls, go on dates or play Guitar Hero on their PlayStations—to gain a slim edge that might pay off with a 70 tomorrow instead of a 71.

At the Academy's 30-acre practice facility, small groups of golfers decamp from the driving range to a short-game green ringed with bunkers. "I want you working on one of three things—pitch, chip or bunker shot, whichever one you have the *lowest* up-and-down percentage on," an instructor called out. A spiky-haired boy practiced full-swing flop shots from heavy rough. He could have killed the girl five yards away had he skulled one, but his flop shots all floated over a bunker, dropped on the fringe and slid toward the hole. Three hundred yards away, another group practiced putting. One youngster was trying to make thirty three-footers in a row. Another was stroking ten-footers, trying to sink ten of fifteen. Other kids stuck tees in the green and aimed at them, trying to hone their putting by shrinking the target. Diligent students, they were emulating the biggest grind of all time. Tiger Woods was known to work on his putting for three hours at a stretch, including an hour in which he practiced his stroke without aiming at a target; an hour of working on distance control, making putts from ten feet, then ten feet and one inch, then ten feet and two inches, and so on; and an hour he gave over to his imagination. In that third hour, he'd line up a putt and say to himself, "This is for the Masters."

"We practice all the time. It's definitely a grind," said Isabelle Lendl, "but it's worth it." Her smile started small and then grew wide and sunny. "When I win!"

Already five foot ten at age fifteen, Isabelle swung, walked and even marked her ball on the green with the grace of a born athlete. No motion wasted. In early 2007, when her older sister Marika couldn't wait to graduate from Pendleton and join Vanderbilt's golf team, Isabelle said college golf sounded like a waste of time. "I want to go pro." Marika liked parties and dances, while Isabelle, to her father's secret pleasure, was more of a golf nerd. Her idea of a party was beating balls while the power chords of the alt-rock band Everclear poured through the earbuds of her iPod. "Isabelle is like Ivan. She's a grinder," said Samantha Lendl, her mother. "She wants to outwork you, and it offends her sense of fairness that some people win without working hard. I tell her talent matters, too. It's work *and* talent. John McEnroe didn't have to be a grinder, but her father did."

Ivan thought he and McEnroe were talented in different ways. "The ability to work hard—isn't that a talent, too?" he asked.

One of the few things Isabelle Lendl liked more than practice was comp—Academy shorthand for competition. She loved the fight and expected to win almost every time. If she was two hundred yards from the hole, she wanted to hit the flag.

"Don't try to be perfect," her father warned her.

"Why shouldn't I?"

"It's unattainable. You'll disappoint yourself." Thus passes the wisdom of nineteen Grand Slam finals from father to daughter. If only she would hear it. "Nobody can be perfect every shot," Ivan said.

"Nobody *yet*, Dad."

Isabelle had a quality sometimes called "kickassitude." Stronger than mere confidence, less toxic than arrogance, kickassitude is a Tigerish sense that you *deserve* to beat other players into the ground. In Academy lore the term dated back ten years, to when Maria Sharapova was a nine-year-old ten-

nis prodigy at Bollettieri's tennis academy. One day, Bollettieri alumna Martina Hingis, ranked number one in the world,
stopped by. After Hingis graciously rallied with the youngest
girls at the academy, Bollettieri asked each one how it felt to
hit with the Wimbledon champion. *Super*, the girls said. *Awesome!* Until he got to little Sharapova, who said, "I hope she's
still playing when I'm sixteen. I'll kick her ass!"

Few Bradenton golfers ever had more kickassitude than
Paula Creamer, whose pink outfits and fluffy headcovers be-
lied her inner panther. "Paula was born tough," says Gary
Gilchrist, who was the Academy's director when she arrived.
An only child like so many other driven stars, Paula challenged the top boys to skills tests ("I'll hit ten balls closer to
the flag than you") and bet with her instructor ("Putting
contest—five bucks"). After turning pro at eighteen she won
the 2005 Sybase Classic, becoming the second-youngest winner in LPGA history. But she made bigger news at that year's
Tour Championship. Paired with Annika Sorenstam as they
played the final hole, the rookie called a rules violation on
Sorenstam. They argued on national television. Paula lost the
argument and the tournament, but she never backed down.
Two hundred miles away in Bradenton, Academy kids watching on TV cheered their heads off.

One of Creamer's classmates was pint-sized Julieta
Granada, who came from Paraguay in 2001. Her father, a
greenkeeper, stayed home in Asunción while she and her
mother moved to Bradenton. Julieta, whom everyone called
Juli—pronounced Hooley—learned English by watching sit-
coms in the cramped apartment she shared with her mom.
They couldn't afford a car, so Rosa Granada bought a pair of

bicycles that she and her daughter rode to the range, the golf course and the Bradenton Wal-Mart. Rosa had a saying: "Enjoy the sacrifice."

Only five foot two, gritty Juli drilled range balls until she could hit nine out of ten of her modest 230-yard drives within five yards of each other. "You'd show up in the fog at first light, and there'd be two kids hitting balls," says Gilchrist. "Paula and Julieta. That's grit."

Julieta fought her way through the junior and amateur ranks to the Futures Tour, the LPGA's version of the men's minor-league Nationwide Tour. In 2005, she won the Futures Tour's YWCA Classic. That title was worth $10,500, which went a long way at Wal-Mart. Still she drilled balls every morning on Leadbetter's range, practicing for hours while her pint-size white poodle, Bimba, watched.

In November 2006, Julieta had a shot at a victory worth nearly one hundred times as much as the YWCA Classic: the LPGA's ADT Championship at Trump International Golf Club in West Palm Beach. The trophy was a plastic cube packed with ten thousand crisp hundred-dollar bills. With her mother carrying her clubs (they had yet to hire a pro caddie), Julieta held off Lorena Ochoa and Karrie Webb to claim the first million-dollar prize in women's golf history.

Adios, bicicleta. Juli bought a white Range Rover Sport. To her delight, the SUV responded to voice commands in Spanish. The Rover became a familiar sight beside Leadbetter's private-lesson tee at ChampionsGate, parked beside Charles Howell's black Escalade with its *CH3* plates.

"Julieta is proof that great toughness can be more important than size or strength," Leadbetter said. Compared to Michelle Wie, who was a foot taller and far stronger, Julieta might seem to have no chance. But she had gone from the Academy to the pros the right way, one patient step at a time. By the time she reached the LPGA tour, she was ready to win.

A few weeks after her ADT triumph, Julieta was filling in behind the cash register at the ChampionsGate pro shop. A pair of loud, middle-aged golfers blew through the door. "Where's Lead?" one bellowed. "Where's Ernie? I haven't seen any pros. Where's Charlie Howell?"

Juli couldn't help herself. "I'm a pro," she said.

"Oh yeah? What did you ever win?"

"A million dollars."

Isabelle Lendl might be the best Academy female since Paula Creamer and Julieta Granada. After she closed one tournament round with a birdie, her father lugged his folding chair to the parking lot and tossed it into his long-suffering Infiniti sports van. "Isabelle contends I pick on her. She may be right," he said.

Ivan felt he had to be tougher on Isabelle. Her sister Marika was headed for college, so she had more time to get her game together. But if Isabelle was to turn pro instead of going to college, she had to learn faster.

"When Isabelle was eleven, I gave her a homework assignment," Ivan said. "At that time she hit her best three-wood 150 yards. I said, 'Here's your situation: You've got 140 over water to reach the green. Think it over—I want you to figure out your average score if you go for the green, and your average score if you lay up.' So she went off and thought about my question. Finally she comes back with her answer:

She figures she would clear the water twenty times out of one hundred. She figures she would average 4.8 on the hole when she laid up, versus 5.2 when she goes for the green. The lesson is obvious: She should lay up.

"That very weekend, in a tournament, she has the exact shot we were talking about: 150 over water. And she goes for it! Of course she knocks it in the drink and I'm about to hang myself. Unbelievable! After the round I said to her, 'Isabelle, what were you thinking? You told me you could hit that shot only twenty times out of a hundred.' And she said, 'I thought it was gonna be one of those twenty times.'"

Four years later, Isabelle played the percentages more often. As good as she was, there were twenty or thirty other teens who could beat her on any given weekend. "Even when I'm hitting it great, winning a tournament, there's some girl playing great who's right on my butt," she said.

That day she stood ninth among 1,851 nationally ranked girls in *Golfweek*'s junior rankings. (The main ranking systems, including *Golfweek*'s list and the AJGA's Polo Golf Rankings, are updated sporadically; I have used the ranking that made the most sense at the time.) Peter Uihlein was number one among 5,899 boys. Almost all of those 7,750 juniors golfers spent at least two hours a day honing their swings. Many saw school, nongolf travel and dating as distractions. Even religion could be pushed aside. One Leadbetter Academy golfer was a devout Catholic, an altar boy, until he decided the time he'd been spending in church could better be spent on the range. Still, there was no guarantee that all this grit would pay off. In fact it was a long, bumpy road from even the highest level of junior golf to the pro tours. Of the ten boys who were junior All-Americans in 1997, not one was on the PGA Tour in 2007. Of the fifty-seven who made All-American or at least honorable mention that year, only four were Tour players ten years later. The odds were better for girls: Of the forty-one female All-Americans and honorable mentions of 1997, six were on the LPGA Tour a decade later. As for the premier golf school on earth, its record was mixed. Only a handful of Leadbetter Academy players had reached the PGA Tour. Several, including Ty Tryon and David Gossett, had made the big Tour only to flunk off as fast as they arrived. Two Leadbetter girls, Paula Creamer and Julieta Granada, had won the LPGA Rookie of the Year award, but after a dozen years in business the Academy still had plenty to prove.

Leadbetter told me there was more to the Academy than turning out pro golfers. His players often landed college scholarships: $177,000 in scholarship dollars for the class of 2004, and twice that for the class of 2005. (Still, those scholarship dollars amounted to no more than $10,000 per recipient, a return of less than a dime per dollar of their parents' investment.) Academy alums might also reap benefits in the corporate world, he said: "Good golf can be a big help in the business world. A player might get a job because the boss is a golf nut."

But perhaps the main reason to attend the Academy was to keep up with other driven kids. "I don't how they do it," said one Leadbetter dad, puzzled by his golfaholic son's desire to hit ball after ball after ball, "but I know *why* they do it—my boy and the rest of the real American kids. They're always looking over their shoulder. They can't relax because they know some other kid is hitting balls. Probably a Korean kid."

The Republic of Korea has 50 million citizens and 250 golf courses—fewer courses than Ohio. A golf boom began there during the 1988–1993 presidency of Roh Tae-Woo. Unfortunately, he pushed an American idea of golf as a sport for the upper crust, rather than following the lead of Scotland, Sweden or Australia, where the game was more egalitarian. The same would soon happen in China. In the land we call South Korea, country clubs charged $500,000 to join and daily-fee courses cost $200 a round. Still South Korea went golf-crazy, and the craze accelerated in July 1998, when Se Ri Pak won the U.S. Women's Open. Korean news accounts of that day feature this term: 뇌성 대명. It means "a name heard around the world."

Se Ri Pak had a cold, hard youth. Her father, a former nightclub bouncer named Joon Chul Park, heard there was money in women's golf. He made his daughter run up and down stairs, forward and backward: fifteen flights forward to build her leg muscles, fifteen flights backward to make her conquer her fear of falling. He woke her at dawn to take practice swings beside her bed. In the winter he supervised outdoor practice sessions, Se Ri hitting balls until icicles hung from her hair. To toughen her mind he made her walk home in the dark, past burial grounds that were said to be haunted. He made her watch pit bulls fight to the death. Se Ri wondered if other children worked so hard. She didn't know much about other children; she seldom played with them. Only against them. As a golfer, she won every amateur tournament in sight. She was fearless.

After coming to America to study with Leadbetter, Se Ri Pak won the LPGA's 1998 Rookie of the Year award. (Her surname is a typo, a U.S. immigration agent's misprint of "Park." She was too shy to object, and soon so famous as "Pak" that she figured the name was good luck.) To meet her then was to be dazzled by her athleticism and hundred-watt smile. Her triumphs in that year's Women's Open and LPGA Championship inspired younger Koreans to dream of becoming world-renowned golfers. "But I dreamed it first. Or maybe my dad did," she told *Golf Digest*. In Korea, she said, "Parents are always watching. You have to be the best. Be number one! Number one! And you think someday you'll have more fun."

Pak was the only Korean player on the U.S. women's tour in 1998. Less than a decade later there would be forty-five, including fifteen who were rookies in 2007. The so-called "Seoul sisters" looked up to Pak the way American golfers once idolized Arnold Palmer. Many were pushed by fathers who saw Joon Chul Park as a genius, men who believed that relentless training would turn their daughters into wealthy, world-famous golfers. Such a plan worked for the Korean women's archery team, which didn't compete in the Olympics until 1988, and then took every individual and team gold medal in the Games from 1988 through 2004. Korea's female archers endured mountain climbs with weights on their backs, mopping up sewage and being marched through a crematory. The same tactics didn't work as well in men's sports—the talent pool for men was so deep that fierce training made less difference. But what came to be called "extreme practice" seemed to work for girls, in golf as well as in archery and other sports. Starting in the late 1990s, tens of thousands of Se Ri Pak wannabes headed for Korea's cramped, jam-packed driving ranges, followed closely by their parents. Thus began a war of attrition, with golf balls for ammunition.

If a Korean girl hit 300 balls in a day, a respectable number for a U.S. Tour pro, her neighbor on the range might hit 400. The next player down might hit 500, a commonplace total at Seoul's triple- and quadruple-deck ranges, where one teen won a bet by beating 1,500 balls in a day. "In Korea, young girls routinely practice eight or ten hours a day, seven days a week," says Leadbetter, who runs an Academy outpost at Woojeong Hills Country Club, near Seoul. "They go to school for half a day every two weeks, the legal requirement." Most pound balls at space-saving "chicken cage" ranges where their drives plop into tubes of green nylon mesh. With golf so expensive to play, many Korean golfers don't play. They only practice. At Woojeong Hills, one lucky fifteen-year-old whose parents belong to a club follows this program: Up at 5:00 a.m. to do schoolwork; school from 7:30 to 12:30; lunch in the car on the way to the range; hitting balls from 1:30 to 3:30; on-course practice from 3:30 to 7:00; putting practice from 7:00 to 10:00; working out in the gym from 10:30 to 11:00; home at midnight. Every three weeks, she gets a day off.

The Korean method has introduced a level of grit that raised the stakes for everyone in junior golf. Its successes are there for all to see. Birdie Kim, a Leadbetter teen who changed her name from Ju-Yun Kim for luck, made birdie by holing a bunker shot on the last green to win the 2005 U.S. Women's Open. A year later, Koreans won eleven LPGA tournaments, sweeping more than a third of the tour schedule. Se Ri Pak, still only twenty-eight, claimed her twenty-fourth victory and fifth major. At the end of the year she joined Nancy Lopez, Annika Sorenstam, Babe Didrikson Zaharias and twenty others in the LPGA Hall of Fame. By then Pak was hailed as Korea's godmother of golf, a national heroine. She was also a famous burnout case. Worn down by injuries and twenty-five years of joyless golf, she wanted to quit. "I hate to be on the golf course," she admitted.

The twins Aree and Naree Song, who grew up in Bangkok, were two of Se Ri Pak's spiritual sisters. Their Korean father, In-Jong Song, wanted to strengthen their legs, so he sent them to school every day with sandbags strapped to their ankles. Each night at bedtime, each girl had to promise their father that she, not her sister, would be the number-one golfer in the world. After she turned pro in 2003, Aree got an e-mail from their father:

> **I am so proud of you for surviving, but it does not stop right here...I still have to wear a villain's mask, to advise you with methods that will push the envelope in your and Naree's skill set...To be a true winner you need to drop more sweats...I always wanted to be like other fathers who are devoted and caring, spending more time with their kids and [taking] them often to fun trips... you and your sister will eventually judge and evaluate my role as your father.**

He was no villain compared to a few of his countrymen. During one tournament, the LPGA pro Soo Young Moon's father reportedly threw her golf bag at her. In Florida, a Korean-American boy begged an opponent to let him cheat: "If I shoot 85, my dad will beat me up." The other player told tournament officials, and the Korean-American boy was disqualified, last seen being led off the course by his dad. And according to sources who spoke confidentially, one Korean father got so angry at his daughter that he grabbed her nineiron and beat her with it, breaking her arm.

In 2003, when I was editor of *Golf* magazine, I sent interviewer Peter Kessler to talk with a woman who had once been the game's pinup girl. After their interview, Kessler called to say, "Wait till you hear this." The voice on Kessler's tape belonged to Jan Stephenson. In her Aussie accent, the fiftyone-year-old Stephenson said, "This is probably going to get me in trouble, but the Asians are killing our tour. Absolutely killing it."

It was my job to run that quote or kill it.

Stephenson was the first to say publicly what others said in private: that some of the young Korean pros were hurting the tour's PR efforts. Strangers in a strange land, the Seoul sisters could appear chilly to fans and standoffish to their proam partners, corporate bigwigs who paid thousands of dollars to play a round with an LPGA pro. Stephenson went on to criticize Asian players' "lack of emotion, their refusal to speak English. . . . They rarely speak. We have two-day pro-ams where people are paying a lot of money to play with us, and they say hello and goodbye."

Her views were impolitic but not crazy. The "Asian invasion" of the LPGA was a popular topic of golf gossip. But nobody had been reckless or biased enough to rip Asian players in print. I knew that publishing Stephenson's quote would get her in trouble, but ran it anyway because it was news. In the tempest that followed, one of the more popular players in LPGA history was demonized as a racist. She backpedaled for two days, but there was no escape. Only public penance would do. "I would like to express my deepest apologies to the Asian community for my comments," she announced, still lumping Korean, Thai, Japanese and Chinese golfers into one melting pot. "By no means did I intend to hurt anyone, nor were the statements racially motivated. I sincerely hope you can find it in your hearts to forgive me."

After the Stephenson flap, the LPGA began quietly addressing her concerns. The tour hired a Korean-born liaison to help Korean players with their English. At several tournaments, the Seoul sisters sipped free drinks and mingled with corporate sponsors, nibbling kimchi. When reports surfaced of Korean fathers giving illegal advice and kicking a ball or two out of trouble, LPGA commissioner Ty Votaw called a Koreans-only meeting to chasten the fathers, who promptly shaped up. Still, *Golf Digest*'s year-end list of newsmakers featured the notorious Seoul dads: "Some said it was cultural misunderstanding, some said it was jealous players envious of the Korean success and others said it was real problems caused by dads with dollar signs in their eyes." At that point, though, the storm was spent. Votaw's diplomacy helped defuse the powder keg. Today, no one talks of Asian golfers' "killing" anything but the occasional drive. Which doesn't mean that Korean golf prodigies have it easy in America.

Seon-Hwa Lee, a chunky golfer from Chonan, South Korea, began hitting hundreds of balls a day at age eight. She turned pro at fourteen. Four years later she moved with her parents from Korea to Florida without speaking a word of English. She struggled at first, nodding and smiling to pro-am partners, worrying that she'd never fit in. She was entranced by Orlando's Millenia Mall and its enormous parking lot, which suggested to her the wide-open spaces of America. But the mall, her family and the Oreos she loved were about all she had aside from golf. At twenty, she had never gone out on a date. This wasn't unusual: Many of the LPGA's Korean players lived and traveled with parents who saw dating as a dangerous distraction. One Korean mother told her pro-golfer daughter she was welcome to have a boyfriend—after she won the U.S. Open.

In 2006, Seon-Hwa Lee won the LPGA's Louise Suggs Rookie of the Year award. Along with the honor came a task that scared her: She would have to give an acceptance speech at the tour's annual dinner at Mar-a-Lago, Donald Trump's mansion in West Palm Beach. Lee prepared with the same grit she brought to the range and the course. She spent three weeks practicing a three-minute speech in English. At the dinner, wearing a black cocktail dress and spike heels instead of shorts and Softspikes, the twenty-year-old stood up to face a crowd that included Pak, Annika Sorenstam, Hall of Famer Suggs and the new LPGA commissioner, Carolyn Bivens. She spoke in quiet, halting English, pausing to thank her parents, pausing to cry. When she finished, the crowd stood and cheered.

Six months after her acceptance speech, Seon-Hwa Lee was still looking for acceptance. Her swing coach, Mike Bender, had spent weeks trying to get her an instruction segment on the Golf Channel. He got nowhere. "I said, 'This is a great young player.' But they said, 'No way. Nobody cares,'" Bender said. "They didn't want this Korean girl, even if she was the Rookie of the Year."

A Golf Channel spokesman, Dan Higgins, told me it didn't happen that way: "We would never say that." He confirmed, however, that Korean pros with limited English might be a tough sell.

"That's their problem. They should embrace these girls," Bender said. "Why? Because pretty soon the LPGA tour will be 70 percent Korean."

Golf parents all over America worry that an Asian invasion will kill their kids' chances. Boys and girls of Korean, Thai, Japanese and Chinese ancestry now occupy about a quarter of the top spots in the junior-golf rankings. "How can regular kids keep up?" one Anglo-American dad asked me. "American kids aren't going to hit balls ten hours a day. We might as well say, 'Okay, Asia, you win. Take the trophy.'"

At a junior event in Virginia, Don Wilshire watched his daughter, Megan, play in a threesome behind Simin Feng, Annie Park and Julie Yang. Wilshire, a club pro from Kentucky, said, "Nothing against 'em, but I'm a patriot. Look around here. How many Asian faces do you see, and how many American? On our turf!"

Anglo parents often accuse Asian and Asian-American parents of giving their kids illegal help. Both Asians and Caucasians sometimes provide illegal advice by giving their children subtle hand signals. Four fingers might mean "Hit a four-iron," while a thumb turned one way or the other might suggest how a putt will break. "Some parents are pretty slick," says a junior-golf official. "Their signals are subtle, but to the kid it's as vehement as shouting." Junior-golf galleries are so sparse that some moms and dads get away with more direct interference: A parent who hustles over a hill into the rough can often kick a ball without being seen.

According to several insiders, Asian parents are overrepresented among the ball kickers. "They don't have our golf traditions," says Gary Van Sickle, a *Sports Illustrated* writer and junior-golf dad. "In their culture, kicking a ball is like throwing a spitball in baseball. Anything goes if you get away with it."

Each side in this culture clash has its complaints. Asian parents are often shocked by the cursing and club-slamming of American juniors, including one particularly foul-mouthed boy ranked in the top fifteen. "And we get singled out for suspicion! We can't even speak our own language," says Jenny Hu. "If I tell Mu 'Good shot' in Chinese, they can say I gave advice." In fact, one Anglo dad told me some Asian parents were "famous" for giving illegal advice and even kicking their kids' bad shot out of the rough. I kept an eye on Mu's parents during a round at one tournament, and not once did either of them get within ten yards of his ball.

Still it seems Asian and Asian-American parents—Korean fathers most of all—cause more than their share of trouble. "You have to know how to deal with them," says Les Brown, a junior-golf official in Florida. "If there's conflict, you have to be diplomatic. Indirect. When one dad kicked his kid's ball out of a hazard, I called them both in. I looked the father in the eye and said, 'I *know* you'd never kick a ball to a better lie.' He was horribly embarrassed that I said this in front of his kid. And he never tried it again. But then I had a worse one— a real cheater, a dad who carried balls marked like the balls his daughter played, so he could drop one in a safe spot if she hit a ball out of bounds. I don't think the girl ever knew. I called them both in and said, 'I *know* you'd never do that.' And he quit it.

"That girl's on the LPGA now."

A banner over the gate at Sarabande Country Club in Howey-in-the-Hills, Florida, salutes MASTERS CHAMPION ZACH JOHNSON. Johnson, who faced down Woods one Sunday evening to win the 2007 Masters, is swing coach Mike Bender's top client. But most of Bender's students are Korean, like Seon-Hwa Lee, the Rookie of the Year he tried to get on the Golf Channel. And this modest little club half an hour from Orlando is where Bender opened America's first school for Korean golfers.

On a May morning, the air was peppered with lovebugs— large gnats that spend their whole adult lives mating. Love bugs zigzag through the air, stuck together, because the male and female can't agree on which way to go. The kids at the Mike Bender Golf Academy at Sarabande think love bugs are pretty funny. The kids are all from South Korea.

"This is a smaller version of what Leadbetter has," Bender said. Smaller by almost two hundred kids, since Bender had only eight students, but he was sure his all-Korean academy would grow. It offered high-tech training, a small school

(English was the only academic subject) and Seoul food. The lunch menu featured kalbi and bi bim bop, a dish that sounded like a golf bet but was actually rice, beef and vegetables served in a hot stone bowl. Bender pictured his brand-new school as the outlet for a pipeline stretching 7,500 miles to Seoul. Unlike the Leadbetter Academy, which emphasized the college scholarships its players often earn, the Mike Bender Golf Academy touted itself as a halfway house for future pros. There were four classroom courses for young golfers: English, Public Relations, Golf Etiquette and Speaking Training, which Bender's brochure said "will be tremendously beneficial when they enter a professional circuit."

A palm-shaded office building held classrooms and a weight room full of treadmills, physio balls and one girlish touch, a gym mat festooned with wide-eyed Hamtori hamsters. The sound of well-struck golf balls led me from there to a practice range that was nothing like the pristine range at the Leadbetter Academy. Here the grass was thin with bare patches of dirt and weeds. Players aimed at dusty orange traffic cones.

"In Korea, it is not this nice," said Joseph Shin, one of Bender's five instructors. Square-jawed, dressed all in white, he came from Seoul five years ago. Now he used the toe of his white-on-white shoe to nudge a ball onto a tuft of brown grass. At least it was grass. "In Korea, you hit off mats. Always mats."

Asked which Bender Academy player had the brightest future, he nodded toward a girl with a butter-smooth swing.

Annie Park was twelve. She had braces on her teeth. At five foot six she looked almost fully grown, with thick strong legs like Se Ri Pak's. Those legs powered a swing that made

Annie one of the best twelve-year-old golfers in the world. But her upper body was "only average," she said. "That's my problem." That's why she reported to the weight room at 6:30 every morning for hour-long workouts designed to build her core and shoulder muscles. After that she spent hours hitting balls on the range.

"I can hit five hundred balls. I can hit six hundred. I don't mind," she said between swings. "Whatever it takes. I want to make the LPGA. I want to win a couple tournaments and after that, play against the men."

Annie said she wanted to be a winner like Annika Sorenstam and Lorena Ochoa. But what about Michelle Wie? Didn't she want to be like Michelle?

"No. It's not Korean or American that matters to me," Annie said. "It's *golfer*."

A thousand miles from Florida, America's top young chef looked out the window of his restaurant. "Junior golf is littered with burnouts. I was one of them," said David Chang, former Virginia junior champion, former golfer.

There was snow on the ground in New York. Chang was remembering how his golf-mad Korean father taught him to play, back home in Vienna, Virginia. "Oh, my dad loved the game. He said I would be a 'great golf professional.'" At age twelve, Chang took lessons at the Tournament Players Club at Avenel. He played AJGA events, winning and advancing until he ran up against boys who were as driven as he was, including a thirteen-year-old who handed out business cards. "For years you beat the crap out of everybody. Then you move up and it dawns on you that some kids are *so much better*.

That's hard on your self-image. It turned me into a head case."

Chang's most memorable moment came at a U.S. Junior Amateur qualifier. He was four over par through the first eighteen holes. "Bad rounds bugged me. I hated disappointing my dad. So in the second round, I started making bogeys, then triples and quads. I shot 120. Literally a 120! That was the day I quit golf."

He horrified his father by going to culinary school, where he was surprised to find that his golf background helped. "People think cooking is inspiration, but it's mostly practice and hard work, like golf. It's a craft you hone day in and day out." After studying in London and Tokyo he landed work as a line cook at Café Boulud in New York. In 2004, thanks to a loan from his forgiving father, he opened his own place, Momofuku Noodle Bar. It was an instant sensation. *The New York Times* called Chang "an ambassador of celestial ramen noodles and all things porcine." After launching two more restaurants, he won his industry's rookie-of-the-year trophy: the James Beard Foundation's 2007 Rising Star Award for Best New Chef. Chang was the hottest young chef in America, but he was still thinking about golf.

"Korean culture and golf are a weird mix. It's depressing to think of all the Korean kids out there, hitting a billion balls." At twenty-nine, he has a golfer's thick forearms and a chef's knife-scarred hands. "I was just good enough to see how many levels there are—how *great* you have to be to play professionally. Unless you're a total junior legend like Tiger or Phil, the odds are so long. I knew some great AJGA stars, and for years I expected to see them on TV, but they all disappeared. Now they're club pros or equipment reps, if they stayed in the game. Fans don't think about all the guys teaching lessons, all the guys on minitours—what heroes they were as juniors! If the kids at golf academies knew how long the odds are, they'd cry. I'd like to tell them, 'Have fun! Play other sports, too. Live a life.' Do you think they'd ever listen?"

THREE

TEACHING: THE SCIENCE OF
SWINGING A STICK

David Leadbetter owes his career to a nasty case of asthma. He was born in 1952 in Worthing, a briny town on the English Channel. His father, Douglas, a former RAF captain, sold farming supplies while gawky David fought for breath on the playing fields of Sussex. Other kids jeered at the Leadbetter boy, who was so skinny his breastbone stuck out at a visible angle. There were days when he couldn't find the breath to run. On those days he sat and watched the others, studying the ways they moved.

David was seven when his father moved the family to Africa. Douglas Leadbetter hoped the climate of sunny Rhodesia would aid his son's health. And the boy grew stronger, displaying a surprising, storky grace on the cricket pitch and tennis court. Still, his asthma dogged him. He would be talking to a friend when his hand would fly up and wave—his way of calling time-out while he suffered a minute-long bout of chest-wracking coughs. That still happens: Leadbetter will be chatting with a Tour pro or an autograph-seeker when the coughs hit him, his hand flies up, calling time, and he remembers why he chose a game that doesn't make you run.

Nick Price, a boyhood friend who would be Leadbetter's first famous student, recalls Lead as a decent player—a bit of a klutz, but studious. The teenaged Leadbetter was Rhodesia's bookwormiest golfer, says Price, "always with his nose in a book." Most often it was Ben Hogan's 1957 *Five Lessons: The Modern Fundamentals of Golf.* But the budding guru also pored over Percy Boomer's seminal *On Learning Golf.* He read about Ernest Jones, a one-legged Englishman who gave five-dollar lessons at a golf studio on New York's Fifth Avenue in the 1920s. He read up on Alex Morrison, the original "golf coach to the stars," who taught Babe Ruth and Bing Crosby and made early swing-sequence photos by having a golfer swing in a dark room with a lantern hung from the neck of his driver. The young Lead took lessons from South African teacher Phil Ritson, but most of his ideas came from books, and *Five Lessons* was his Pentateuch. Reading Hogan's words, he pictured the glum little scientist digging wisdom out of divots. Looking up from the book to watch other golfers swing, Leadbetter saw Hogan's fundamentals in action. The swing began to look like a set of interlocking gears.

"Other teachers saw the same stuff later, after video came in, but David saw it with his own eyes," says Price, "because David can see in slow motion."

Golfers from Price and Greg Norman to Michelle Wie

and Mu Hu believe Leadbetter has a sixth sense: He sees the myriad pieces of the swing all at once.

Maybe he inherited that sixth sense. Leadbetter's grandfather George, an English soldier blinded by a German bullet during World War I, went on to become one of England's leading osteopaths despite his handicap. "Cripples came from everywhere to see him," Leadbetter recalled, "and I was entranced by his power, this magic touch he had. Wouldn't it be wonderful to see things other people didn't see, and to use that power to help them?"

Leadbetter studied accounting in college, but his heart wasn't in it. He still dreamed of teeing it up with South Africa's Gary Player and other stars of international golf. Unfortunately for the freckled twenty-year-old with a cranium full of swing thoughts, he was a head case.

Leadbetter would be rolling along, two or three under par, when a crooked shot would send him off the rails. "I threw some clubs. I broke a few over my knee, and tore a few gloves in half." Storky Lead was no natural athlete, and it was a triumph of intellect that he nearly made it to the European Tour in the first place. A triumph that felt like a curse, because what's worse than knowing exactly how to hit a shot and then missing it? Betrayed by his body again!

His best chance came in the European Tour's qualifying tournament in 1976. Last day, back nine: He seemed to have no chance until he flew a nine-iron into the cup for an eagle, then birdied the next hole. One final birdie and he would earn his tour card. "The last hole was a par-five. I played it sensibly—laid up and hit a pitch to twelve feet. I can still see the putt. It broke a little, right to left...and rolled over the right edge." Thirty-one years later, picturing that twelve-foot putt, he still expects the ball to break a half inch more. But rather than break the putter over his knee, he slipped it into his bag and turned his back on the tour. Now he sees that day as the beginning of his adulthood. "Fate deals you a hand," he says. "I wasn't meant to be a player."

Back home in Rhodesia, he worked at a driving range. After a later stint teaching lessons in England, he chased his fate all the way to Chicago, where the twenty-six-year-old Leadbetter arrived in 1979 as the new assistant pro at Oak Park Country Club.

"It was cold in Chicago!" He lived in a cramped couple of rooms in the club. The bathroom down the hall was rancid. "Absolutely appalling. So at night I'd sneak into the ladies' locker room, where the bathroom was quite nice. But my trespassing brought down the wrath of Millie." Millie was an apparently two-hundred-year-old club employee who guarded the ladies' lair with a zeal worthy of the Chicago police. She swore she would catch the sneak who showered and shaved in the ladies' room.

"One night I had a date with a member's daughter. Club members are always trying to marry their girls off to the golf pro. I was showering in the ladies' room when there came a banging on the door. 'We know you're in there!' I jumped out of the shower, dripping, climbed out the window and made my way back my room. Got dressed and walked out to see a half dozen people outside the ladies' locker room. 'We've caught the perpetrator!' Millie cried. I had left the water running, so they thought the fiend was still in there, showering."

In 1980, Leadbetter fled to Florida's Grenelefe Resort,

where he taught at the Andy Bean Golf Studio for $15 a lesson. Most of the work was the old-time elbow-straight, head-down religion. He was itching to try out his evolving thoughts on swing science, but who would listen to a no-name pro who wanted golfers to quit using their hands?

Traditional teaching held that power came from the legs, control from the hands. The germ of Leadbetter's theory, which built on the work of teachers including Ernest Jones, Alex Morrison and John Jacobs, was that traditional teaching was doubly wrong. Leadbetter suspected that a perfect swing would minimize both leg thrust and hand action. Power was best generated not by the legs but by torque—twisting and untwisting the large muscles of the torso. Hands were too tricky to trust under pressure—they'd double-cross you.

The "classical" swing of the game's golden age emphasized arms and hands, but he came to see that view as a relic of the age of hickory shafts. Golf's hickory era, which lasted into the 1930s, was all about controlling that whippy, almost rubbery wooden shaft, using the hands and arms to make last-second adjustments that squared the clubface at impact. "When steel shafts came in, the great Byron Nelson saw how they would change the game. Nelson focused on lower-body movement with *less hands*, because the small muscles of the hands will betray you under pressure," says Leadbetter, who began picturing a swing that synchronized arms and body in one fell swoop. The Leadbetter swing would quiet the hands and let the twisting torso do the work. The golfer would be less like an artist, more like a machine.

What he needed was world-class players to test his ideas. Unluckily for Lead, there was no call for golf gurus in 1980. With rare exceptions like Player, a so-called fitness freak, Tour pros tended to be lazy, out of shape. They trusted instinct over theory.

Have a look at a PGA Tour practice range in 1980. It wasn't pretty. There was power in Jack Nicklaus's controlled lunge, his hands and elbows riding high as his lower body surged forward, but that swing wouldn't work for you. Nor would Craig Stadler's rhythmic walrus wallop. Arnold Palmer was still out there, still strong as a blacksmith, slashing away with a huge hip turn and looping follow-through. Lee Trevino, looking like a slicer's nightmare with his open stance and outside-in approach, somehow contrived to hit a modified block that faded gently to ground in the heart of the fairway, but his approach was too quirky to teach anyone else. A few pros turned to teachers now and then: Nicklaus took advice from Jack Grout, who had coached the Golden Bear since he was a cub in Columbus, Ohio. Others relied on Bob Toski or Jimmy Ballard. But in 1980 a Tour player's entourage still consisted of his caddie. Pros wouldn't dream of bringing swing coaches with them on the road. What were they, sissies? When young Leadbetter told an interviewer that Trevino's swing was a mess—"a mess that *works*"—the six-time major winner snarled, "Show me a coach who can beat me and I'll work with him."

Leadbetter couldn't beat Lee Trevino. But he could teach someone else to do it. What he needed was an avatar. Or better yet, a couple of them. A couple of Nicks.

Nicholas Raymond Liege Price, five years younger than Leadbetter, was another Rhodesian who gravitated to the European Tour and then to America. Both became Zimbabweans in 1980, when their homeland was reborn with a Shona name that means "big stone house." Price was nothing like the scrawny Lead. A poster-boy jock, he was a water-skier with stone-hard muscles and the sandy coif of a pop star. He was also a born ballstriker. Even after Price won the 1974 World Junior title as a seventeen-year-old, he had no idea how his swing worked. Eight years later, frustrated by his lack of progress as a pro, he remembered his old acquaintance.

Now charging a robust $30 a lesson, Leadbetter made the most of his cramped quarters at Grenelefe. He would tape Price's swing, then hustle to a closet-sized room where a secretary sat answering phones. She rolled her swivel chair into the hall to make room for Leadbetter and Price, who paid no attention to the phones. "We had a clunky first-generation camcorder and a monitor," a Leadbetter assistant recalls. "David used a grease pencil to draw swing-plane lines right on the monitor's screen." As Leadbetter stopped and started the image, the video verified what he had seen with his slow-motion eye: Price's torso muscles whipping his arms to impact, hands and club going along for the ride.

Along with grease pencils, rulers and protractors, the Leadbetter crew kept a stack of air-sickness bags in their little video room—a jokey reminder that it can be sickening to see yourself swing. "I didn't realize how badly I swung the club," said Price. He headed back to the range. Not for an hour or a day, but for more than two solid weeks.

"David kept me out there for six hours a day, sixteen days in a row," Price says. His torturer, golf's Torquemada, made him hit up to one thousand balls a day. All eight-irons. "We used those giant buckets that held two hundred fifty balls. I would empty three or four of them in a day. Eight-iron, eight-iron, eight-iron. He said there was no point hitting other clubs until I hit this one right. I literally wore a hole in the face of my eight-iron." Price kept at it because he began to feel his swing getting tighter. He had been a marginal player because his distance control was spotty—he'd hit an eight-iron 150 yards one day and 130 the next. "Now I was hitting shots that practically came down one on top of the other."

During Price's trial by eight-iron, Leadbetter lightened the mood with practical jokes. "One night he slipped into my room and painted all my fingernails green," Price says. Leadbetter also gave his victim a green mustache.

A week or so later, Price's mustache and manicure had faded, along with his old habits. His hands were hard-callused and his ballstriking was otherworldly. Now Leadbetter introduced a new drill. Kneeling, he flipped golf balls that Price hit with a baseball bat. The drill reinforced a crucial concept: "The hips lead the backswing, Nick."

"The hips are tired. The hips hurt!"

"The hips lead the backswing. Swing, batter!"

Looking back, Leadbetter says, "Nick was a great talent and a great guinea pig."

That summer at Royal Troon, four months after laying his game at Lead's feet, Price led the 1982 British Open by three shots with six holes to play. "They're not going to catch me now," he told his caddie. The golf gods hated hearing that. A rotten bounce, a double bogey, another bogey and before he knew it Price had lost by a stroke. He would admit he hadn't been ready to win a major. He lacked two prerequisites: a swing so perfectly repeatable it could withstand Sunday-afternoon Open Championship pressure, and the steely self-regard he saw in Tom Watson, who beat him that day.

Price outdueled Jack Nicklaus to win the 1983 World Series of Golf, but his swing remained a work in progress. He and Lead were learning that keeping a swing grooved is as hard as grooving one. It helped that they had video, which isn't only for spotting errors. It also records good swings for future reference. If Price lost his swing, as golfers do, he could find it again in the video room. Watching his best swings—Nick's greatest hits—not only helped him fix technical flaws; it also got his head buzzing in the best possible way. He and Lead didn't know it yet, but watching video was activating mirror neurons in Price's brain. Seeing the right move was a form of practice; it helped him repeat the move the next time he swung.

Still, Price didn't win again for eight years. Nor did he switch coaches, which makes him one of the stubbornest guinea pigs in sports history. Each winter, before the golf season began, he wrote the same thing in his diary:

"Persistence. Persistence. Persistence."

In 1992, Price turned thirty-five. It had been eighteen years since he won the Junior World Championship. Sixty-three majors had been played since he turned pro in 1977 and he had won none. But after a decade's worth of Leadbetter lessons, he knew he was a better player than the one who lost to Watson at Troon.

The 1992 PGA Championship proved him right. Price's three-stroke victory kicked off a three-year run in which he was the best golfer in the world. Not just the best ballstriker but the best *player*, his mind, his swing and his soul working like interlocking gears. In 1993 and 1994, Price was the PGA Tour's Player of the Year. In 1994, his best year, his six victories included the British Open and the PGA. And yet he wasn't Leadbetter's leading student, or even his leading Nick.

Nicholas Alexander Faldo came from Welwyn Garden City, the shredded-wheat capital of England. Like the town's main export he was seen by many as abrasive and tasteless.

Faldo had been a quizzical child. When his parents gave him a bicycle for Christmas, he took a wrench and dismantled it to see how it worked. He grew tall and broad-shouldered, handsome in a blank sort of way, like a man hiding dark thoughts. At twenty-one, he was England's top golfer. The English press treated him with hot- and cold-running passion, cheering his triumphs and jeering the collapses that earned him a Fleet Street nickname he hated: "Foldo." After folding down the stretch at the 1983 British Open and 1984 Masters, he turned his analytical mind inward and didn't like what he found. "A little voice in my head said, 'You ain't got it, mate.'" After quizzing Price about Leadbetter's theories, he made the same decision Price had made. He would dismantle his swing and rebuild it. Swallowing his considerable pride, he turned himself over to Lead.

"Throw the book at me," Faldo said.

Leadbetter had a look at a golfer with blazing ambition and a fine, nearly musical tempo. But his swing was practically the opposite of the one Leadbetter taught. He slid his lower body toward the target on the downswing, making last-instant compensations with his wrists and hands to deliver a pure strike. Lead was impressed by those talented hands—it took skill to compete at the game's highest level while essentially improvising every swing. Yet he agreed with Faldo's self-diagnosis: Such a move worked well enough Thursday through Saturday, but it would melt in the heat of a major-championship Sunday.

Lead warned the pride of English golf that remaking his "armsy-handsy-legsy action" would be hard work. It might take a year. It might take two years.

"I don't care how long it takes. I am sick of playing mediocre golf," Faldo said.

The guru put him on a program that made Price's boot camp seem like high tea. After weeks on the range and video sessions that left the monitor covered with grease-pencil lines, Leadbetter got Faldo to stand up straighter so he could rotate rather than sliding. A flying elbow was grounded by flattening the left wrist at the top. Then Faldo beat balls until the bandages and tape over his blisters were caked with blood. Some days he emptied four 250-ball jumbo buckets, then dragged another to his station on the range and made his way through that one, too. He soaked up instruction—the more technical the better. "Faldo was a madman for technique," another pro says. "If you said a move should feel 'smooth' he'd look at you like you were talking Chinese. But if you said 'left arm at forty-five degrees,' he'd do it. Not forty-six or forty-four—forty-five degrees."

One tenet of Leadbetter's teaching was that the body must be trained. You can't have the mind sending orders to the body, because pressure makes the mind babble. The teacher's job, then, is to help his player forge a swing that is muscle memory incarnate. To do it, Leadbetter used more than video, lessons and buckets of balls. He used gimmicks. He made Faldo toss medicine balls. He had him swing with fishing rods. He bound Faldo's knees with thick rubber bands. He also accompanied him to Tour events, where Leadbetter was usually the only swing coach to be seen. "Nick's Nanny," some pros called him. Other players got a laugh watching Faldo endure one of Lead's leg-strengthening drills, hitting drives with a basketball between his knees.

Faldo kept playing tournaments and kept playing worse. Now, rather than folding on Sunday, he missed cuts on Friday. In 1986 he had to rally at the season-ending Walt Disney World Classic to keep his PGA Tour card. "Those were dark days. The papers back home were giving me hell," Faldo says. "I'd been Europe's number one before changing my swing, and here I was working like a madman, hitting a thousand balls a day, with no results." Leadbetter told him to keep the faith. "You're almost there," he said. "All the work you've done is gonna pay off." The unproven guru was so sure he was right that when Faldo hired a new caddie, Fanny Sunesson, Lead made her take a seven-week course in the Leadbetter Method.

In July of 1987, Leadbetter flattened Faldo's swing a few extra degrees to prepare him for the British Open at Muirfield, Scotland. He would need to hit the ball low. When chilly winds swept off the Firth of Forth on Sunday, July 19—the day after Faldo's thirtieth birthday—he was ready. Still, everyone but his coach expected him to fold after he finished three rounds in second place, a single shot off the lead. On

Sunday morning a Scottish bookmaker offered favorable odds on Faldo, hoping to draw some action, but it didn't work. Three hundred bettors placed wagers with the bookmaker that day, and not one took Faldo at 5–1.

Playing in the twosome ahead of leader Paul Azinger, Faldo kept the ball low in a stiffening breeze. He made par after par. Azinger was clinging to a three-stroke edge as they made the turn.

Facing a long approach to the par-four 10th, Azinger asked for his one-iron. His caddie, Kevin Woodward, talked him out of it. As fate would have it, this was the same caddie who had toted Price's bag at Troon five years before, when Price bragged, "They're not going to catch me now." Woodward was determined to bring his man home a winner this time. Knowing Azinger was practically jumping out of his skin, pumped with adrenaline enough to hit the ball ten extra yards, Woodward handed him his two-iron. Azinger slashed his approach into a greenside bunker. Bogey. Rattled, he three-putted the next green— his only three-putt of the week. Another bogey. Meanwhile, Faldo was swinging like a metronome. Par, par, par. At the 17th hole, Azinger drove into a fairway bunker. Had his hand muscles twitched? Another bogey. They were tied.

A hole ahead, Faldo stood on the last green, forty feet from the hole. He had kept his mental blinders on all day, seeing nothing but the next shot. Now, though, after four days and 277 strokes, he allowed himself a flashback. He thought back to his boyhood, to golden afternoons in Welwyn Garden City when he would size up putts like this one and hear an imaginary announcer: "Faldo has this putt for the Open Championship…"

He drew his putter back and then forward, sending the ball on its way.

Maybe his flashback threw off his concentration. Maybe his fingers betrayed him. He watched with mounting panic as the ball ran four feet past the hole. After seventeen pars, this! Azinger standing in the fairway with a five-iron in his hand, Faldo a longish short putt from a foldo his Fleet Street critics would never let him forget.

His four-foot comebacker would get him into a playoff if Azinger parred. It would win him the Claret Jug if Azinger bogeyed. But if he missed…

"Hit it firm," he thought. "Hit it solid and it will hold the line. Bang it in."

In it went. Faldo's lower body nearly slid out from under him, not from poor technique but from relief. He let out the breath he didn't know he'd been holding. And when Azinger pulled his five-iron into a bunker and finished with yet another bogey, Nick Faldo was the Open champion. Minutes later he was smooching the Claret Jug and telling the world he owed his success to David Leadbetter.

"The greatest credit goes to David. He remade my swing," Faldo told reporters, recounting his long, bloody days and months on the range. "When I began working with David it was very, very hard, like walking backward all your life and then learning to walk forward. I went through pain barriers. But today proved it was all worth it." This was the gracious Faldo, a man Leadbetter knew but few others ever saw. Nice Nick was sincerely grateful to the man he dubbed "Lord Lead." He could have patted himself on the back for his breakthrough at Muirfield. He could have taken sole credit for the triumphs to come—a ten-year run as the best golfer on earth, a decade in which he claimed two more Open titles and three Masters victories and was justly praised as the toughest pressure player in the game. Instead he credited Lead every chance he got, and Leadbetter's phone began ringing. Could Lord Lead have a look at another Tour pro or two or three or ten?

Faldo made a proud return to Muirfield in 1992, winning yet another British Open. That evening he kissed off his old Fleet Street enemies, saying, "I just want to thank the press from the heart of my bottom." By then he was the closest thing golf had to a rock star. Faldo partied with musicians Elton John and Phil Collins. After a round he would shoulder his way through a buffet line, grab a hunk of meat and gnaw it like Henry VIII. He played practice rounds alone and dined with his agent because nobody else liked him much. He insisted that Leadbetter meet him at Tour events as if Lead were Nick's roadie. Faldo demanded unstinting attention from Lead but didn't want to pay for it. In their first years together, he paid Leadbetter $20,000 a year to rebuild his game and chase him around the world, coaching and praising him, massaging his ego as well as his swing. That number never went up. Since Lead paid his own travel expenses, he actually lost money working with Faldo, who earned more than $4 million in the nineties.

"I didn't mind," Leadbetter says. "He was the reason people knew who I was. And you have to admire the guy— Nick Faldo was really the instigator of the modern game." There was no precedent for what Faldo did with Leadbetter: physical training, mental training, the hard work every pro now accepts as part of the job. "Sure, Jack Nicklaus was a hard worker, but that was another era. Like Arnie and everyone before him, Jack practiced by *playing the course*. Faldo changed all that by training like a real athlete."

Leadbetter soon found himself racing to keep up with a growing band of golfers who wanted to train the same way. Keeping his Nicks apart was a juggling act in itself. Price, one of the most affable stars in any sport, loathed the self-centered Faldo, so their sessions had to be scheduled hours apart. The juggling got still more complex after Faldo destroyed Greg Norman at the 1996 Masters, a defeat that made the loser rethink his career and turn to Leadbetter, who was now the game's best-known teacher.

Norman may have been cursed with too much talent. "Greg had serious swing problems for years, but was such a brilliant athlete he'd make the right adjustments at impact," Leadbetter says. "The trouble is, that doesn't work under extreme pressure. You just unravel." After Norman dropped swing coach Butch Harmon for Lead, there were three future Hall of Famers beating balls on the range at Lake Nona, an Orlando resort that became Leadbetter's base in 1989. Nice-guy Price could only shake his head as Norman grumbled about their coach's focus on Faldo, while Faldo resented the newcomer. "Faldo and Norman were like schoolgirls, worrying that Lead liked the other one better," one insider recalls. Leadbetter hustled to keep his stars happy while tutoring a dozen other Tour pros and tending to his burgeoning business of instructional books and videos, magazine features, infomercials and a new academy for junior golfers in Bradenton. He often ran so far behind schedule that his nickname was amended. His assistants called him "The Late Lord Lead."

Business boomed. Faldo seethed. Though Leadbetter

spent more time with him than with all his other Tour pros combined, it wasn't enough for prickly Faldo, who had a few nicknames of his own. Golfers he snubbed called him "Nasty Nick" or "Nick the Prick."

By any name he was no longer the workhorse who once hit five hundred balls a day. "He'd lost focus," says Leadbetter. "He was having personal problems." In fact the forty-year-old Faldo was in the process of dumping his second wife, Gill, for a twenty-year-old golfer named Brenna Cepelak. According to a Lake Nona instructor, "Nick was focused on Brenna. She would show up on the range and be all over him. Then they'd disappear into the hotel for a couple hours."

At the same time, Lead's father was dying. Douglas Leadbetter had skin cancer—likely due to his years in the African sun he'd hoped would cure David's asthma. (Lead's Panama hat is no mere trademark; along with the sunblock he slathers on, it shields him from the rays that struck down his father.) Douglas died in the summer of 1998. Faldo still wanted Lead to join him at the upcoming PGA Championship at Sahalee Country Club in Redmond, Washington. Instead, Leadbetter flew home to England to spend two weeks with his mother. Faldo finished fifty-fourth in the PGA, then heard that his coach had been seen with another client, Se Ri Pak, at the Women's British Open.

"It was true. I was already in England, so I drove to the ladies' Open for a day. I gather Nick didn't like that," Leadbetter says.

Soon he got a letter from Faldo. "A Dear John letter," he calls it. "*Your services are no longer required. I need to go in another direction.* I'll admit I was hurt. After thirteen years together, he didn't bother to pick up the phone."

The guru had learned a lesson: At the game's highest level, personality, loyalty and money could matter as much as technique. Within a year, Faldo signed a multimillion-dollar deal with Marriott Hotels to open a chain of Nick Faldo Golf Institutes—including one in Orlando, just up the road from Lake Nona—where "certified instructors" would teach students to swing "the Faldo Way."

Setting up a golf school is no gimme. Fortunately for Faldo, his teacher had shown the way. The golf school's modern evolution began in the eighties, when Leadbetter and several other brand-name teachers reinvented the way the game was taught. Like exercise gurus and porn czars, they did it with videotape.

Until the eighties there were almost as many swing theories as there were teaching pros. You could talk golfers into jogging to the ball and hitting it on the run; or hitting putts with their eyes shut; or using a "non-backswing swing" that started at the top, with the player frozen like a statue in mid-swing. All three of those tricks were tried, with only minor injuries. After video's arrival, however, voodoo morphed into something more like science. As Leadbetter and his lieutenants dissected the swing in stop-motion, grease-penciling angles and numbers on the monitor in their video closet, the measurable similarities in players' swings suggested a new paradigm.

"Teaching golf is like forensic science," Leadbetter says. "You're a detective looking for clues." The first videos helped debunk several truisms that turned out to be false. Keep your head down? No—your swing will be too stiff. Keep your left arm straight? Not perfectly straight, or you can't make a full turn. Video confirmed Leadbetter's belief that sliding the lower body toward the target was the wrong way to generate power, since that slide forced golfers to make last-instant adjustments—a prescription for erratic play. Worst of all, the classic legsy-handsy swing tended to implode under pressure, when the hands' many muscles literally shivered, turning muscle memory into muscle schizophrenia, a malady familiar to every duffer who ever tried to correct his slice in the last nervous inch of his downswing.

Leadbetter taught a more reliable swing. In the Leadbetter motion, which grew out of his own observations and the teachings of earlier swing coaches, the legs and hands go along for the ride—a ride driven by a violent twisting of the torso. This brave new swing called for muscle and timing. It demanded the strength to accelerate the clubhead to 100 mph or more, and the timing to synchronize torque with the whip-like motion of the arms and club. But when it worked, it was as quick and strong as lightning.

"We were all thrilled to be part of it," says Steve Wakulsky, one of five Leadbetter instructors working with Leadbetter after Faldo made him famous. Wakulsky was a marginal player, what he himself calls "a minor leaguer making a few dollars on the J.C. Goosie Space Coast Tour." "That's when David's phone started ringing off the hook—he had dozens, *hundreds* of people wanting to take lessons from the great Leadbetter. He couldn't give lessons to everyone who wanted them. There weren't enough hours in the week. I loved David's passion for decoding the golf swing, so I basically quit playing to help him create a training program. And it was the most valuable time of my life. We developed a way to teach David's philosophy even if David was on a plane to Hawaii or Hong Kong."

For starters, Leadbetter taught that most swing flaws occur in the first quarter of the swing. Even today his lessons with Tour pros including Trevor Immelman and Charles Howell III start with a close look at their address positions. In Lead's view, every good swing begins with a stable, balanced setup. From there, the small circle of torso rotation drives the bigger circle of the clubhead's arc, with the arms and club connecting the two.

"The swing is like a wheel turning: The outer rim moves faster than the hub," says Wakulsky. Intense and professorial, he speaks so precisely you can almost hear the punctuation. "Our job is to get the outer rim, the clubhead, moving in time with the hub. That's the key to a powerful, repeatable swing." Force is created by twisting body parts, with the shoulders turning more than the hips—a difference that creates torque. "The shoulder turn should about double that of the hips. Normal numbers would be a ninety-degree shoulder turn and a forty-five-degree hip turn." At the moment of transition, the lower body begins shifting forward while the upper body tarries an instant, completing the backswing. This tension, familiar to anyone who has cracked a whip, adds force that travels through the arms and shaft to the clubhead. "Swing segmentation at the transition builds torque, then the arms and club unload force through the ball. You finish with your weight on your left heel, your right heel off the ground and your right knee moving into your left knee."

Got that? It is the simplest description of the Leadbetter

swing. Or, for that matter, the swing most modern instructors teach, now that Lead and other name-brand gurus have spent twenty years refining it. The difference is in the details—innumerable variations that depend on a player's size, shape, strength, flexibility and personality. Diagnosing flaws and prescribing remedies add more variables. And that's only for the full swing. We haven't yet gotten to pitching, chipping, sand play and putting.

As Leadbetter refined his gears-and-angles view of the full swing, including the perfect positions he identified from setup to follow-through—his "Eleven Links"—he sometimes overwhelmed students with information. "He could drive you absolutely stark, staring mad, and I say that with love," says former touring pro David Feherty, now a TV golf analyst. "You didn't know if you were taking a lesson or taking calculus."

Leadbetter admits he got carried away. "I had to learn to feed the knowledge intravenously, a little at a time."

In the early 1990s, with help from Wakulsky and a few others, he drew up a training manual. As it grew to and then one hundred pages it became an indispensable field guide for a network of certified Leadbetter instructors all over the world. The manual has a long official name, but everyone calls it the Workbook. Now 125 pages long, it opens with this line: "Congratulations! You are about to embark on the David Leadbetter Golf Academy's Instructor Training Program." For a young teaching pro, this is a bit like reading, "Congratulations! Welcome to the Navy SEALs." You take a deep breath before turning the page.

The Workbook is a Leadbetter trainee's bible. He must sign for his copy and protect it carefully during the year of his training, the way NFL players guard their playbooks. "This program is one of the key factors that differentiate the DLGA from all the other golf instruction schools and training institutions," the Workbook announces on its second page. That's no idle boast. With its lesson plans, charts, tests, required-reading lists and 328 drills, the Workbook provides quality control throughout Lord Lead's empire. It allows an instructor in France or Thailand to give his students most of what they'd get if they flew to Orlando and paid the CEO rate of $50,000 a day for the boss's attention.

The Workbook's introduction gives a few basic rules. Trainees must carry a notebook at all times, to record their trainers' tips. They are never to put their hands in their pockets (you look sloppy) or look at their watches during a lesson (you look bored). They must memorize a branching diagram showing nine kinds of ball flight, from a pull hook on the far left to a push slice on the right. They must study Leadbetter's bestseller *The Golf Swing* and answer questions including "Many people try to totally eliminate the use of hands and wrists—is that what David intended?" and "How did David suggest you control the length of sand shots?" (Answers: No; By the length of your follow-through). They must master the Eleven Links from address, Link 1, through backswing, Links 2-5, to follow-through, Link 11. They must cut a DVD of themselves demonstrating all eleven, review the DVD with their local trainer and send it to the Director of Training and Certification in Orlando. At this point they have reached page twenty-four of the 125-page Workbook.

Leadbetter is famously fond of quirky training aids, from his Faldo-flustering beach balls and basketballs to hula hoops and eye patches. The heart of the Workbook is a cornucopia of drills. Some are clever, some sound screwy, but all 328 drills have passed muster over years of teaching, even "Squeeze a Nerfball Between Your Thighs." Try it—you'll make a fuller turn.

One look at the Workbook suggests the myriad ways a golf swing can go wrong. There are eighty-six backswing drills to cure such ills as *Faulty Weight Transfer* and the dreaded *Reverse Pivot*. There are seven drills for the crucial moment of transition. There are thirteen for a common downswing flaw, *Over the Top with the Right Side*, including one, "Hit balls with the right eye closed," that keeps instructors on their toes lest they get plunked by mis-hits. Another seventy-five "Miscellaneous Tips" cover everything from *Poor Balance* to *Shanking* to *Putting, Chipping and Pitching*. Trainees must know every drill in the book. They prove their mastery by teaching novice golfers whose swings are taped before they begin lessons, taped again during drills and yet again after lessons have improved their swings. Nothing is left to chance—the Workbook even devotes one and a half pages to directions on how to film the swing, with face-on and down-the-line views as well as shots from behind the player. In a sidenote, it allows trainees to skip the rear view in some cases: "For women, by request only, eliminate this view." Who says chivalry is dead?

For years, trainees' tapes were FedExed to Leadbetter headquarters. Today they are digitized and e-mailed for instant review. The feedback continues after trainees become certified Leadbetter Instructors, earning embossed business cards and the traditional chocolate Certification Cake. Since nobody has yet figured out how to digitize cake, the cards and

Two-year-old Tiger Woods and his father, Earl, on TV's *The Mike Douglas Show* in 1978, with Douglas, Bob Hope and James Stewart

The security gate at the IMG Academies campus in Bradenton, Florida

Kevin Cook

Young golfers can train on several greens on the Leadbetter Academy's 30-acre practice range.

The 300-acre IMG Academies grounds feature apartments, a nature preserve, a spa, an on-campus school and a golf course.

Academy Park

A Double-Ended Golf Range
B Short Game Area
C Baseball Fields
D Academy Park Villas
E Soccer Offices / Locker Rooms
F Soccer Fields
G Academy Park Tennis Courts
   (3 Hard Courts & 7 Clay Courts)
H Golf Offices

IMGA Campus

1 31 Hard Tennis Courts
2 9 Clay Tennis Courts
3 Adult Activity Center / Massage
4 Sports Performance Center / Mental
   Conditioning / Junior Recreation
   Center / Game On
5 Stadium Hard Court
6 Admissions / Executive / Basketball /
   Tennis
7 Stadium Clay Court
8 Mailroom
9 Bollettieri Resort Villas
10 Health Services
11 Junior Reception / Transportation /
   Proshop / Junior Cafeteria / Bank / Sales /
   Operations / Snack Machines / Travel Offices
12 Junior Pool
13 Student Services / Computer Lab
14 Basketball Courts
15 Sports Therapy
16 IPI Weight room / Offices
17 IPI Turf Training Field
18 Indoor Tennis Center (4 Courts)
19 Pendleton / University of Miami
20 Pendleton Classrooms
21 Clubhouse Reception
22 Pool / Jacuzzi
23 Rental Lodge
24 Spa

Golf Course

47th Street West

Nature Preserve

34th Street West

Titleist scion Peter Uihlein was one of America's top junior players.

Arnond "Bank" Vongvanij liked to hit the ball high.

Instructor Tim Sheredy worked with Isabelle Lendl.

The golfing Lendls:
Ivan with daughters
Isabelle (left), Marika
(center) and Daniela,
aka Crash

Darren Carroll

Powerful Charlie
Winegardner used
a baseball-style
grip.

Nick Price choppered
in for a lesson with
Leadbetter.

Kevin Cook

eadbetter in a rare quiet moment, in his office at ChampionsGate

cottish phenom Carly Booth had her doubts
out the teaching she got at the Academy.

Preacher's son Michael Wade would swing so hard his hat would fly off.

Mu Hu, the golf star from Shenzhen, China

Leadbetter wanted Mu to hone his short game.

Michelle Wie struggled to live up to her old form in 2007.

Leadbetter and company stripped the swing to bare bones in his swing lab.

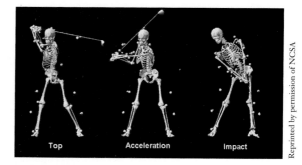

Top   Acceleration   Impact

Former phenom Ty Tryon spent the year playing minor-league golf.

Sean O'Hair at the PGA Tour's 2008 PODS Championship, which he went on to win

England's Oscar Sharpe, the new boy wonder at the Leadbetter Academy

cake go out by snail mail. Today there are sixty Leadbetter Instructors based at twenty-five resorts in eleven countries, with ten to twenty trainees moving through the Workbook at any given time. "We're in constant touch by e-mail, watching lessons our instructors teach and updating the instructors on David's work, which never stops," says Wakulsky, who produced the Workbook's seventh edition in 2006. "Every month I make a DVD of David with a prominent client and post it for all our people to see." A Leadbetter instructor in Marrakesh clicks on a link and watches Lead working on the takeaway with Charles Howell III—"Charlie Three-Sticks," they call him—or showing Ernie Els a new downswing drill.

"I like to use a medical analogy," Wakulsky said. "Think of a small-town doctor, dedicated but alone. Then think of the Mayo Clinic. We're the Mayo Clinic. We're a network of experts with David at the hub, driving the whole thing as it evolves."

The Workbook was famously technical—too technical, some said. For years, the only knock on Leadbetter has been that he focuses so much on technique that "Leadbetter golfers" lack confidence and creativity—the intangibles that rescue a player's round on the days when his swing springs a few leaks. Critics said Lead's quest to perfect the full swing produced robotic golfers who tended to go haywire under pressure, as Howell, Els and Michelle Wie had been doing too often. Still, the Workbook was perfect for IMG. It provided a ready-made blueprint for a golf school.

When IMG decided to add a golf academy to its sprawling facility in Bradenton, the mega-agency turned to Leadbetter, who was already an IMG client. And Lead was intrigued by the thought of creating a school for young golfers. With his method and IMG's money, he thought, they might change junior golf forever.

Way back in the 1970s, Nick Bollettieri had an idea. "A boarding school for tennis! I'll give kids a college experience," he said, "but they won't major in English or business, they'll major in *great*." In 1978, Bollettieri, a fast-talking hustler from New York, opened a tennis school in Sarasota, Florida. His first students got a college experience, all right. They bunked eight to a room and ate junk.

There were no dorms, just a pair of rented houses. "Half the kids lived in my house. We fed 'em peanut butter sandwiches and lemonade. Sometimes baloney. For dinner, pizza." Bollettieri was forty-six at the time, but he could outhustle teenagers. "I'd get up at four in the morning. I'd wake the kids up at dawn and drill 'em with my three D's: dedication, desire, determination!"

His school shared tennis courts with a sleepy local resort. The Colony Beach & Tennis Club's graying guests didn't enjoy dodging Nick's kids, who zoomed around the grounds chasing each other's overhead smashes, grunting and spitting and cussing. The kids were soon banished to a remote row of courts where they couldn't bother anyone. But come five o'clock, when the older folks were sipping cocktails on the deck by the clubhouse, Bollettieri would bring his phenoms to the front courts and put on a show. *Bam* went the aces, *bam* the crosscourt bullets, and before you knew it the oldsters were bringing their grandchildren to the Nick Bollettieri Tennis Academy.

Students paid $1,500 a month for tuition, room and board. It was never quite enough to cover expenses—not with Nick giving free rides to prodigies like Andre Agassi and using every spare dollar to grow the school. When a friend loaned him $50,000, he used the money to buy the crumbling Manatee Court West Motel. For weeks his tennis coaches scrubbed mildewy bathrooms and Stygian toilets. One coach nailed wooden planks over the windows to keep the students from escaping. Players slept in bunk beds, still eight kids to a room. The tallest boy slept with his feet hanging out between the planks of a bedroom window.

"OK, it wasn't the Ritz," says Bollettieri. In 1982 he talked two wealthy friends into loaning him $2 million. A businessman would have banked at least some of the money. Bollettieri bought a tomato farm. The farm was in Bradenton, a sunburnt burg up the road from Sarasota. He rented a bulldozer and leveled chocolate-colored fields where tomatoes and gardenias had grown, making room for dorms, offices, a cafeteria, a gym and acres of tennis courts.

In those days, when corn still grew across the fence from the academy, Bollettieri's prize pupil was a scrawny kid from Las Vegas. Like many if not most phenoms, Andre Agassi was the child of a domineering father. Mike Agassi, a burly casino worker at the MGM Grand, hung tennis balls over his son's crib when Andre was a baby. By the time the boy was six, Mike had him out on the court, hitting three thousand balls a day. Andre was thirteen when he turned up at Bollettieri's school—a grunter who could drill passing shots past pros twice his age. Powder a first serve and he'd smack it back harder. A rock 'n' roll jock who dyed his shoulder-length hair rainbow colors, Agassi sometimes wore eyeliner and a touch of lipstick on the court. On a campus where alcohol was forbidden, he built a 6-foot pyramid of airline-size Jack Daniel's bottles in his dorm room.

Bollettieri looked the other way. He bent the rules for stars like Agassi, Boris Becker, Martina Hingis, Monica Seles, Venus and Serena Williams and Maria Sharapova, who would all reach number one in the world. They would all earn multimillions while Bollettieri remained a thousandaire, barely breaking even on the world's top tennis school. Agassi dumped Bollettieri in 1986 and went on to earn more than $50 million on and off the court while Bollettieri, who had schooled him for nothing, got nothing.

In 1987 Bollettieri sold his academy and campus to IMG for $7 million. "I coulda handled my money better," he told me. "I gave too many scholarships. I gave the business away. So I had to sell it." He stayed on to run the tennis school that bears his name. Twenty years later, Bollettieri, seventy-six, was still there every weekday, a trim, leather-skinned man who spoke in a leathery growl. He no longer woke at four in the morning; as a concession to age, he slept in until 4:20. His first lesson began at 5:30 a.m.; his last ended at 7:00 p.m. Then he drove home to Cindi, his eighth wife.

"I was always reluctant to bring in other sports, but IMG wasn't," he says. "And when you think of it, golf's ideal for the sort of intensive training we started here. It's like tennis—nobody's knocking you on your ass, so you can focus on the ball."

In the early nineties, IMG had the same thought. "At that time the Leadbetter operation was a pretty typical resort program," says Ted Meekma, a Bollettieri protégé who went on to be an IMG vice president. "You'd take a couple lessons, play a round of golf, have a nice weekend, go home with a shirt. David saw promise in the model we'd built for tennis, and he had what we needed: a unique instructor-certification program."

The David Leadbetter Golf Academy opened in Bradenton in 1994. Its six students included a boy from the Czech Republic who had never played golf. His parents just wanted a golfer in the family. With Gary Gilchrist running the school on a day-to-day basis, the Bradenton half dozen practiced on a dilapidated range with a trailer park on one side and an All-U-Can-Eat oyster bar on the other. The chubby Gilchrist was louder and pushier than Lead: less of a sage, more of a fighter. He knew—everyone knew—that tennis was the big game on IMG's Bradenton campus. He planned to take the big game down a peg. "I saw how the tennis players trained, and saw that this would be the way in golf," he says. "We'd all been told golfers reach their peak at age thirty. But if we could accelerate the learning curve so they peaked far younger, we could do even better than the tennis academy."

What began as a new wrinkle in coaching—using deputies to teach the Leadbetter swing—was developing into something more ambitious. Along with the junior academy in Bradenton, Lead's operation soon featured a space-age swing lab at ChampionsGate, where precision was measured in millimeters, degrees and pounds per square inch. The short-game practice range at ChampionsGate had targets at 50 and 100 yards but also at 48, 63, 87 and 90. A grassy circle served as target for another sort of precision landing: It was a helipad for Leadbetter clients Nick Price and Greg Norman, who

choppered in for lessons. Price, Norman and Lead's younger
Tour players got a closer look than the juniors at Bradenton.
The main objective in teaching juniors was to make the Leadbetter swing automatic through repetition, but Tour players
already had near-perfect swings. In his work with them, the
guru's task—after a quick check of their alignment and address position—was to offer tweaks that might add a yard to
the seven-iron or, more important, a one-percent increase in
distance control. If he could help Charles Howell III or
Trevor Immelman land the ball a foot closer to the hole, those
young stars might break into the top rank of Tour pros.

The small clubhouse behind the ChampionsGate range
held racks of Leadbetter books and DVDs as well as hats,
sunglasses, sunblock and jumbo cans of Performance Protein
Plus diet powder. The walls were hung with magazine covers
and signed photos of Price, Norman, Ernie Els, Arnold
Palmer, Jack Nicklaus and other clients, all inscribed with
fond messages to Leadbetter. Down the hall was Instruction
Bay #1, where many of the guru's students had scrawled
their names on Lead's Wall of Fame. Pride of place went to
Norman, whose autograph was two feet higher than the
rest: *David, thanks my friend, Greg Norman.* Below that were
scribbles from Els, Nicklaus (*The old man could use some help*),
Charles Howell III, Annika Sorenstam, Justin Rose, Camilo
Villegas, Bernhard Langer (*God Bless You*) and Aaron Bad-
deley as well as Alice Cooper, Peyton Manning and Halle
Berry (*I'm golfing because of you!*). Michelle Wie wrote *Mahalo*,
Hawaiian for "thank you."

Leadbetter had lucrative endorsement deals with Rolex,
Cadillac, Callaway, SAP software and half a dozen other firms.
A star of DVDs and infomercials seen worldwide, he was more

famous than most of his clients. He stood second to Butch Harmon on *Golf Digest*'s list of golf's 50 Greatest Teachers, a ranking that rankled a bit. Lead was more expensive than Harmon: In 2007 they both charged $50,000 for a one-day clinic, but Harmon gave an occasional one-hour lesson for $600 while Leadbetter commanded $10,000 for a half day's instruction. Insiders said Harmon was less "technical" than Lead, but that was a shade of difference at most, since Harmon had been technical enough to revamp Tiger Woods's swing. Harmon taught a big swing, a wide, capacious arc that boomed the ball forward, while Leadbetter stressed timing—the sequenced unfolding of a swing driven by the twisting muscles of the torso, with the hands and club going along for the ride. But at this late date in the evolution of the swing, their differences weren't as big as their Web sites suggested. The main difference was style—Harmon the pushy, blue-eyed bulldog versus Leadbetter the cerebral stork. Their rivals included latecomer Hank Haney, whose stock-in-trade was a wide separation of the arms on the backswing. Haney's stock rose when he replaced Harmon as Tiger Woods's coach and helped Woods re-revamp his swing. A second tier of teachers included Rick Smith, who had just lost Phil Mickelson to Harmon; old warhorses Jim Flick and Jim McLean; and newcomers Mike Bennett and Andy Plummer, who were making noise with a swing wrinkle they called "Stack and Tilt." Tour pro Aaron Baddeley had left Leadbetter to work with Bennett and Plummer—the latest blip on the fast-shifting power grid of the PGA Tour, which boosted or dented the top teachers' stock almost daily. Lead might be the best-known golf guru, but he would lose ground if his players defected to Harmon, Haney or Gilchrist, or if the players in his stable didn't win. With Mickelson in

Harmon's camp and Woods working with Haney, Leadbetter needed his pros—Els, Howell, Immelman, Michelle Wie, a dozen others—to make headlines.

The latest addition to Leadbetter's operation was Instruction Bay #2, the swing lab. In here, a few steps down the hall from the Wall of Fame, the walls and doors were shiny black. Floor-to-ceiling curtains damped the thwacks of hard-hit balls. Starting in 2006, Leadbetter had teamed with the University of Pittsburgh Medical Center (UPMC) to see if the UPMC's Neuromuscular Research Lab could shed new light on his swing theories. That new light was already shining. It was infrared.

Today Tim Sell, a sturdy, no-nonsense researcher with a Ph.D. in applied biomechanics, was helping a grad student calibrate eight cameras in Instruction Bay #2. The high-speed infrared cameras, which produced four hundred images per second, were housed in steel cages mounted in the walls. The cages were there to protect the cameras—Ernie Els might never foul off a lens-smashing shank, but Halle Berry might.

"We are measuring the differences between elite golfers and everyone else," Sell says. "If we know how Ernie Els generates ball speed, we can help less proficient players improve."

As golfers hit balls at a net in Instruction Bay #2, Sell's cameras fed 3-D images to a pair of computers. More data came from two stainless-steel force plates under the golfer's feet. Each $10,000 force plate, equipped with four transducers, sent data on weight shift to Sell's computers. The force plates were so sensitive that Sell could check his readouts and tell you which pocket your cell phone was in.

After testing more than six hundred golfers, including

thirty-five PGA Tour pros, Sell and his colleagues showed how everyday hackers lunged at the ball, moving their shoulders, hips and arms all at once, while the best golfers unleashed core-driven power in the three-part downswing Leadbetter prescribed. In a great golf swing, the hips' rotation led the way, pulling the shoulders and then the arms toward the ball. A great swing was more like cracking a whip than swinging a stick. "We've confirmed a lot of what David saw with his naked eye," Sell says. "But we're starting to make some discoveries, too."

One discovery was the crucial role of the hip abductors, a pair of muscles connecting the pelvis to the thighs. Pro golfers' hip abductors were 30 percent stronger than amateurs'. Sell's work also quantified the X factor that measures the torque in a golf swing. A typical duffer's X Factor is 8—he turns his shoulders eight degrees more than his pelvis in the backswing. But a typical pro's is 21. Sell and his UPMC colleagues used their data to create an exercise program for golfers: They took fifteen volunteers with an average handicap of 13. They put their volunteers on a simple, stress-free program: forty-five minutes of strength and flexibility exercises three to four times a week. Two months later, those fifteen golfers had boosted their X Factor by 26 percent and bumped their driving distance from 211 yards to 229.

While only the top-tier juniors were brought to the swing lab at ChampionsGate, they all practiced the "holistic" approach to golf that Leadbetter pioneered. One of its benefits was purely physical: Leadbetter's instructors believed that the boss's approach helped prevent injuries.

A few of them were discussing the evolution of the swing one sunny afternoon. One said there would be no more quirky

moves like Jim Furyk's in another five years. "Not here, anyway!" He admitted that Furyk's herky-jerky swing, which has
been said to resemble an octopus falling from a tree, worked
for Furyk, but suspected that it put too much strain on his
body. "He hurt his wrist, didn't he?"

The great Seve Ballesteros had ruined his back with his
violent lunge at the ball. Many other golfers suffered from
inefficient biomechanics. "A flawed swing doesn't just fail
under pressure. It can physically hurt you," the instructor
insisted. "The Leadbetter swing doesn't hurt you."

Leadbetter's holistic approach extended into players' minds.
"There's only so much you can do with a golfer in an hour-
long lesson," says IMG's Ted Meekma. "But you can do major
surgery in a school year. You can teach a kid how to win."

Once a week, IMG Academies athletes reported to the
Mental Conditioning Center, where golfers worked with as-
sociate director Chris Passarella. His job was to keep them
from tripping over their own brains.

In previous decades, a golfer who admitted getting nervous over a putt might be laughed off the course. It was sissi-
fied to admit you had negative thoughts, or thoughts of any
kind. As Sam Snead said, "When I think, I don't play so
good."

By the twenty-first century, however, psychology was as
much a part of the game as fitness or nutrition. "Golfers are
the humblest of athletes. They're always one swing from ca-
tastrophe," one sports psychologist says. Leadbetter Academy
golfers wrote their worries in notebooks they showed to Pas-

sarella and other mental coaches, who told them not to worry about worrying. In fact it was healthier to say "I'm nervous" than to pretend you weren't.

His view was supported by a study in the journal *Psychological Science*. In the June 2007 study, researchers at UCLA found that simply naming one's fears could help tame them. When subjects described their negative feelings, activity in the brain's emotion-processing center "was calmed." Another new study at England's Hertfordshire University showed that women who tried to suppress cravings for chocolate ate more of it than women who talked about their cravings. Again, it seemed that being mentally honest with yourself was the best policy.

Passarella found that a similar process can help golfers build confidence. Golfers tend to label themselves, to think *I'm streaky* or *I'm a golfer who always has one bad hole*. He challenged Leadbetter kids to make those labels work for them: to pause after a string of pars and think *I'm consistent*, or bear down after a seven, make birdie on the next hole and think *I'm a bounce-back golfer*.

The Academy's mental coaches seldom gave pep talks. They hardly mentioned the Zone, that state of hocus-focus in which everything goes right. The Zone was so-o-o eighties. Leadbetter had a line about how fleeting that feeling could be. "I've got it I had it I lost it," he said, talking fast. Perfect contact was fine while it lasted, he said, but tournaments were won and careers made the other 99.9 percent of the time.

Modern golf psychology had less to do with seeking perfection than with managing imperfection. During talks with the aggressive Peter Uihlein, Passarella said, "Don't worry about results. Don't think, 'I've gotta hit this green, gotta birdie this hole.' Think about process. Think, 'I'm gonna swing *down* to clean contact and pop the divot up.'" Passarella trained golfers to reboot like a computer between shots, using simple routines to help them wipe their minds and focus on the next shot, never the last one. A technical player like Sean O'Hair might use a rigid pre-shot ritual while a feel player could reboot more easily. Tour pro Chris DiMarco did it with a smooth walking pace. Either way, the goal was to steady your breathing.

There was nothing new about that. When *Golf* magazine asked Byron Nelson how he handled pressure during his record eleven-win streak of 1945, Nelson said, "The best way to deal with pressure is to regulate your breathing. You get excited when you breathe faster, and as you breathe faster you swing faster. So you have to slow your walk and take deep, slow breaths." More than sixty years later it appeared that the flip side of rebooting—crashing—was also both mental and physical. Sports psychologist Jim Loehr called choking "a neurological event." The culprit was cortisol, a stress hormone in the brain. Too much cortisol makes a golfer irritable and impatient. His hands get tight, his muscles twitchy. And what's the best way to lower cortisol levels? By keeping your breathing smooth and slow.

At its simplest, much of golf psychology boiled down to this: Breathe deeply, picture your target and pop that divot.

"Of course it's easier said than done," said Meekma. "Some kids never learn to relax under pressure. But others do, and a few of them, a special few, get to where the pressure is the fun part."

Some of the Academy's best battles happened far from any tournament. Leadbetter's lieutenants toughened up their best students by pitting them against each other in intramural showdowns. Tim Sheredy, the instructor who coached many of the school's best players, liked to match his top boys against his top girls on Friday afternoons. The kids played for pizzas and pride, with the winners getting to lord it over the losers all week. Sheredy didn't get paid overtime for his extracurricular matchmaking. All he got was the satisfaction of seeing his best players get better.

In March 2007, he matched Peter Uihlein and Bank Vongvanij against Isabelle Lendl and junior All-American Sydney Burlison. All week, Sheredy needled the girls, telling them, "Peter and Bank say they'll destroy you." All week he goaded the boys, too, saying, "The girls say they're going to kick your butts." He made it all up—neither side was talking smack. But Sheredy wanted his kids stoked for a good fight. As the players took practice swings on the first tee at Legacy Golf Club in Sarasota, he told them where they stood through two previous showdowns: "Boys undefeated—so far."

There was no gallery. Isabelle, two years younger than the other three players, was taller than Syd and Bank and nearly as tall as Peter, the pipe-thin powerhouse who reached the green at the 520-yard 11th hole with a drive and a six-iron. He and Isabelle missed eagle putts there and settled for birdies. That left the boys one-up in a best-ball match in which the sole concession to gender was that Isabelle and Syd used the women's tees—a ten- to fifteen-yard advantage that still left them hitting plenty of hybrid approaches while the boys hit eight- and nine-irons into the greens.

The girls pulled even at the 12th hole, where Isabelle's

twisting birdie putt put her two under par on the back nine. Boys and girls stayed all square until they reached the 16th green, where Isabelle rolled in a twelve-footer to give the girls a one-up lead. She was now five under on the back nine. Peter mimed applause. Isabelle picked her ball from the hole and tossed it at him, but he dodged. "Made you miss," he said.

The last hole was a nasty par-four: 472 yards for the boys, hard wind from the left. For once the women's tees were a long walk forward—enough to even up the muscle difference. "No fair!" said Bank. Swinging hard, he hooked his sky-high drive.

Peter ripped his Titleist to a safe landing. "Good ball," said Isabelle, lacing her drive from the women's tee to the same spot. Peter's 295-yard bomb into the wind had left him 180 to the hole. His seven-iron hopped and stopped twenty feet from the flag. Isabelle's approach was a foot closer. Then Syd bounced a long iron that rolled closer still. The girls were sure to make four—sure to win unless Peter sank his birdie putt.

He wasn't about to leave it short. He plumb-bobbed the putt, conferred with Bank, settled over the ball, took a last look at the hole and finally rolled his Pro V1, one of more than 100 million golf balls his father's company produced in 2007. This one skirted the edge and slipped past the cup.

"Girls win!" said Sheredy.

Isabelle, who had shot 31 on the back nine, crossed the green to where Peter stood bent at the waist, shaking his head. He could not believe he and Bank had lost to a couple of girls. "Good match," she said.

Remembering his manners, he gave her a chaste hug. "Hey, you played great," he said, meaning it. But he couldn't quite swallow losing. After the hug he turned toward the pond by the green, flipped his Titleist into the air and swung his putter at it. Nine out of ten golfers would swing and miss—hitting fungoes with a putter is hard—but Peter Uih-lein made perfect contact. The ball pinged off his putter, flew forty yards and splashed in the hazard.

FOUR

Support: Nobody Makes It Alone

Every junior-golf story is a family story. Most Academy families are upper-middle-class prosperous, with a healthy percentage from the ranks of the wealthy. The Uihlein, Lendl and Hu families, for instance, could water their lawns with Cristal if they chose. A few families struggled to pay for their kids' clubs, lessons, travel and entry fees. Many Academy golfers were only children, watched and pushed and showered with attention. Even those with siblings tended to be the focus of their parents' competitive drive. As psychologist Alvin Rosenfeld puts it, "Parenting has become the most competitive sport in America."

"Parents are a crucial part of the picture, for better or worse," says Leadbetter, who has seen too many kids with talent, grit and fine-tuned swings undone by Mom or, more often, Dad.

In this as in most facets of the modern game, Tiger Woods is Exhibit A. Earl Woods was a dominant figure in Tiger's youth, but not a domineering one. He taught his son the game when Tiger was two years old. (Almost all great players start before the age of ten.) "You must start the learning process when the child is young enough that the performance of the game is totally ingrained and flows from the subconscious," Earl wrote in *Training a Tiger*. He kept practice fun with putting and chipping games, and gave his son constant praise. "Never mention the word *failure*," he wrote. "Always accentuate the positive: 'I like the way you swing the club. It won't be long before you're hitting it a ton!'"

Soon Tiger was phoning his father at work. "Daddy, can I practice with you today?" Earl always paused before answering, to keep his son in suspense. But he always said yes.

Tiger Woods had talent, grit, a well-schooled swing and the best sort of security: the bedrock of loving parental support. "I was never afraid to fail," he has said, "because I knew that I would always come home to a home of love."

Today almost every golf parent cites Earl Woods as a role model. Some, like Ivan Lendl, pore over Earl's books for clues on how to train their own children. Others act so pushy that the overbearing, high-pressure parent is becoming as much a golf cliché as it used to be in tennis. "Half my work is with parents, and most of them don't have a clue," says sports psychologist Jim Loehr. "They push and push until the kid hates golf."

"Sometimes it's a control issue," says Mike Bender. "Do you want to know one reason so many Korean girls turn pro instead of going to college? If they go to college, their parents can't go with them."

"Some parents are delusional," says junior-golf official Les Brown. "Their kid shoots ninety and they blame the greens. They scream at the officials, which is bad, or at their own kid, which is worse."

When Leadbetter worked with Faldo and Price, he was dealing with individuals, grown men who answered to no one but themselves. Today, as junior golf's top teacher, he has to play family counselor as well as coach. "You monitor parents, but you can only intervene up to a point, because they are in control," he says. After all, the parents pay the bills. Argue too much and they'll take their kids to another teacher. "Some don't realize how much pressure they put on their kids—pressure to get points and rankings, to get into the best tournaments, to impress college coaches. It's pressure, pressure, pressure! What's the burnout factor going to be?"

Some parents could recite the numbers that drove them to push their kids ever onward and upward: In 2006, Tiger Woods led the PGA Tour's money list with more than $10 million. He added $87 million in endorsement money from Accenture, Nike and his other sponsors. Even beer-bellied John Daly, who earned only $192,134 on the course in 2006, collected $8 million for sporting the logos of sponsors including Hooters, Dunkin' Donuts and—no joke—TrimSpa. By 2007 even the lowliest PGA Tour rookie could count on $150,000 a year for playing Titleist clubs and balls and wearing a Titleist hat, while a middling pro could command $500,000 a year to put a corporate insignia on his hat, plus

$250,000 or so for wearing a Ford or 84 Lumber logo on his chest pocket.

Golf's money boom had far outstripped the rate of inflation. When Roberto DiVicenzo won the 1967 British Open, he earned £2,100. That was worth about $35,000 in today's dollars. When Woods won the same tournament on the same course in 2006, he earned $1.3 million. The women's tour is less lucrative, with a typical LPGA victory worth about $250,000, yet Michelle Wie and Paula Creamer have proven that even youngsters who haven't won majors can make millions. Creamer earned $1.3 million on the course and more than $4 million from corporate sponsors in 2006, despite a snafu with an endorser that failed to do its homework: One major firm paid big bucks to put its logo on the back of Paula's collar, only to discover that her ponytail covered the logo. She gave that sponsor a mulligan.

Golf didn't get rich just because it is popular. More than any other major sport, it is popular with the right people. The game gets more TV time and commands higher advertising rates than its raw numbers merit because it appeals to a coveted crowd: affluent men. Golf's demographic is catnip to upscale advertisers like Rolex, Accenture and the Royal Bank of Scotland, which have joined Titleist and other golf-equipment companies to bankroll a well-appointed corner of the media landscape. On TV, the Golf Channel prospers. No one ever suggested a Bowling Channel, though there are twice as many bowlers as golfers in America. In the print world, *Sports Illustrated* tried special sections for fans of NFL football, NASCAR and other sports, but only *Golf Plus* drew enough ad dollars to survive. The hunt for upscale advertisers reached a sort of peak in a chart one popular publication sent to advertisers, boasting of its pull with a subset of aging alpha males: *Golf Magazine Is #1 Among Men with Erectile Dysfunction.*

The game was a good fit for the first decade of the new century, a time when the rich grew richer and richer. Only a golf pundit would write a straight-faced line like the one TV golf analyst Johnny Miller gave *Golf Digest* in 2007: "One way I compute inflation is to look at the approximate cost of a Porsche in 1974 ($15,000) versus today ($75,000)." In Miller's world, plenty of families could afford $100,000 a year in Leadbetter Academy tuition and extras. For TV personalities and CEOs, $100,000 was disposable income.

On most days several parents sat in their cars behind the Leadbetter range, where each instructor supervised four or five golfers at a time. Some of the parents watched their children for hours on end. A few used stopwatches to mark the time instructors spent with each golfer, and complained if their kids got less attention than any of the others.

When the Leadbetter Academy was new, in the mid-nineties, moms and dads were welcome to walk the range, but the free-range parent is no more. When the Academy built a new practice facility in 2002, a low hedge was planted between the parking lot and the range to cordon off the parents. But shrubbery wasn't enough to block the pushiest, who went over or around the hedge. And so in the spring of 2007 the range was fenced off with nylon rope like the gallery ropes at golf tournaments. The instructors breathed a little easier.

Nobody wanted to deal with the next Marc O'Hair.

In 1997, the Leadbetter Academy had welcomed a fourteen-year-old recruit named Sean O'Hair, a sandy-haired runt who struck the ball with a fine *thwack* but was skittish as a mouse. Your typical junior-golf star walks with a strut that says, "Hello, world. Meet *me*." This boy moved as if expecting a bomb to go off behind him. He was scared, and Academy director Gary Gilchrist knew why.

Sean's father, Marc, was a bear of a man—six foot three, 260 pounds in a muscle shirt, black cap and sunglasses. Unsmiling, arms crossed, he watched every practice session, every day. When other students said, "Dude, what's up with your dad?" Sean shrugged. All he knew was what his dad drummed into him: "You are going to be a star on the PGA Tour. We are going to be rich." In the meantime, Sean's job was to shut up and play. If he played poorly, he would be punished. If he lipped off, he would be punished. His father, who admired tough-guy football coaches Woody Hayes and Vince Lombardi, made the boy run laps in noonday sun. And that was when he was in a good mood.

The O'Hairs hailed from Lubbock, Texas, where Marc had played quarterback for his high school team. One night he led the squad to a huge upset victory, one family member recalled, but Marc wept while the other boys celebrated. Asked what was wrong, he reportedly wailed, "I should have had two more touchdowns!"

A decade later, Marc taught his son to play golf. Their first playful rounds became something different after Sean showed promise: They became his job. The boy found himself spending hours on the range, drilling balls with teaching pros Marc hired. If Sean complained, he was punished.

For a while, Marc's plan worked. Spindly Sean was one of the top-ranked junior players in Texas before he turned thirteen. So Marc made an investment. He sold his stake in his family's thriving window-shutter business for $2.75 million. "Seed money," he called it, for his next career as his son's manager. Leaving his wife Brenda behind in Texas, he took Sean and moved to Bradenton, where Gilchrist awarded Sean a $100,000 scholarship to the Leadbetter Academy. Sean O'Hair was one of the early phenoms who paid no tuition because their futures looked bright enough to help promote the brand. But his father was trouble from the start. If Sean hit a lousy shot, his father blew his stack. Gilchrist told Marc to back off, but Marc kept pushing.

Steve Elling, who covered golf for the *Orlando Sentinel*, calls Marc O'Hair "the sports dad from hell." On his good days, the man who described himself to Elling as "an iron-asshole bastard" was his son's high-energy helper. On other days, he was Sean's worst enemy. If Sean finished over par at a junior tournament, Marc made him run a mile for every stroke over par. By his own admission, he also hit the boy. "Light slaps," he called them. Never mind that Sean wound up with blood streaming from his nose. As his father explained it, "He has a delicate nose that bleeds very easily."

In his second year in Bradenton, sixteen-year-old Sean grew six inches in six months. Suddenly he was almost as tall as his dad. At six foot one, 150 pounds, Sean was a beanpole with a perfect golf body, but his game regressed while he adjusted to his new physique. He hit the ball farther but played worse. In the second round of a junior tournament that year, he was lining up a putt on the 18th green. He needed to make it to shoot an even-par 72. As he settled over the ball, his father shouted, "If you shoot over par, we're going home!"

Sean missed the putt and Marc made good on his threat. He pulled his son out of the tournament and drove him back to Bradenton. After two years of asking Gilchrist how soon "they" could turn pro, Marc took matters into his own hands.

"I asked him to wait," Gilchrist told me. "Sean had great talent, but he wasn't ready to swim with the sharks. I told Marc they should move up in stages the way Earl and Tiger did. Sean could win the U.S. Amateur. That would get him into the Masters and the other majors, where he could make enough noise to get *big* money when he turned pro a year or two later. But Marc wasn't listening." It didn't matter to Marc that in the previous twenty years only one teenage pro, Germany's Bernhard Langer, had succeeded. Marc thought his boy was better than Langer.

He yanked his son out of the Academy and drew up a pro contract giving Marc O'Hair 10 percent of Sean O'Hair's future earnings for life plus $100,000 for expenses. He showed his son where to sign the papers. Then he filled his Ford Taurus with clubs and golf-training gizmos, luggage and maps, food and a hot plate and took his boy out on the road. Sean's suitcase held a week's worth of clean, neatly pressed trousers. He wasn't allowed to wear shorts or blue jeans because Marc said shorts and jeans were for losers. Sean went along with his father as he always had, out of fear, duty and the passivity his father had knocked into him.

Since he hadn't played his way through the PGA Tour's Q-School, Sean had no status on any pro circuit. He tried Monday-qualifying on the Nike Tour (later renamed the Nationwide Tour) and got nowhere. Monday-qualifying was a great way to gain experience while going broke—battling up to one hundred pros for a handful of spots in a tournament field. Winning a spot was like hitting the lottery, except that the jackpot was most often $0. The "winners" usually missed the cut in the main event, losing out to future Tour stars like Aaron Baddeley and Zach Johnson. In his first full year as a pro, Sean missed cuts in Knoxville, Virginia Beach, Wichita, Dayton and a dozen other towns while Marc put more than 100,000 miles on the Taurus. Sean's earnings that year totaled $1,201. "You need to get stronger," his father would say, heating high-calorie grub on his hot plate in a drab motel room in Boise or Baton Rouge.

Marc woke Sean at 5 every morning and made him run. The rest of the day was for weight lifting and golf, with lights out at 10 p.m. Sean sharpened his ballstriking the way Price had, hitting thousands of balls until the clubface felt like an extension of his body. But whenever he got near the lead in a tournament, he flinched. After he shot 80 one day, Marc made him run eight miles in 93-degree heat, a mile for each stroke over par.

In 2002, TV's *60 Minutes II* aired a segment about Tigermania, showing golf families going all-out to turn their kids into "the next Tiger Woods." On the program, Marc O'Hair declared that being Sean's dad was like running a window-shutter business: "It's material, labor and overhead. He's pretty good labor." He was trying to be funny. That summer, Sean was practicing his putting at the Tournament Players Club in Coral Springs, Florida. A tall, auburn-haired twenty-year-old named Jackie Lucas noticed the thin boy a few yards away. "I tried to get his attention, but it didn't work," she recalls. "He was so shy he'd barely look up." Jackie played for the women's golf team at Florida Atlantic University. Seeing Sean rolling putts like a pro, the ball rotating perfectly end over end like a Steve Nash free throw, she asked, "What tour do you play on?"

Sean couldn't quite bring himself to make eye contact, but he smiled. They talked. Soon they were dating. Two months passed before he worked up the nerve to kiss his first girlfriend. "Sean was more than shy. He was like a robot. A sweet, cute robot," Jackie says.

Marc hadn't counted on this. The last thing he wanted was for Sean to shift his focus from golf to girls. One day when they were on the road, he made a crude comment about Jackie. Sean defended her. They argued. Finally, Sean told his father to "shove it." That was the beginning of the end of the O'Hair family's twisted version of "Father Knows Best."

Tom Winegardner was a more enlightened father, though his hold on his son wasn't exactly welcomed by the boy's instructors. Like Marc O'Hair, Tom had prospered in a family-run business, and like Marc he had a sports background that he saw as a blueprint for his only son's rigorous approach to golf. Lucky for Charlie, his dad was a thinker, not a fighter.

When Charlie Winegardner was in kindergarten, in the mid-1990s, his lanky dad went off to play pro golf. Tom competed with future PGA Tour pros Chad Campbell and Shaun Micheel on the Hooters Tour while his wife, Sharon, stayed home with young Charlie. Sharon couldn't believe her thirty-five-year-old husband would pull such a Peter Pan stunt. "I was so mad at Tom I quit talking to him for a while," she remembers.

In his best week as a pro, Tom qualified for a Nationwide Tour event. A giant step up from the Hooters Tour, the Nationwide is golf's Triple-A circuit. Every year the best Nationwide players graduate to the promised land of the PGA

Tour. Tom led the tournament through Saturday's round, but wasn't up to the challenge of winning. He folded on Sunday and came home with his head hanging. Still Tom thought he could make it as a touring pro. There were better rounds ahead—he could feel it every time he gripped a club. But he would soon be pushing forty, with a wife and child to support. It was time to put his clubs aside. He took a full-time job with his father's General Motors dealerships in Maryland and chased car buyers instead of birdies. Maybe his son would grow up to be the touring pro in the family.

The Winegardners' handsome brick mini-mansion in Lothian, Maryland, was chocked with sports memorabilia: framed Redskins jerseys and a baseball jersey signed by Pete Rose as well as golf posters and paintings. Upstairs, only-child Charlie had two rooms to call his own. One held all the trophies he won in the ten years after his father came home from the Nationwide Tour—rows of baseball, soccer, karate and golf trophies. In a larger room, where Charlie slept and did homework till the middle of his junior year in high school, when he went off to Bradenton, there was a poster showing one of those impossibly hard fantasy par-three holes over the motivational line: *The harder the course, the more rewarding the triumph*. Night after night, Charlie lay in bed with that picturesque par-three on his wall and the first fairway of the Old South Country Club outside his window. The Winegardners were members at Old South as well as at Congressional Country Club in Bethesda, but it was at Old South, right outside the back door, that Tom taught his boy to hold a golf club with a baseball grip and fling the clubhead through impact with audible force.

Dad's hand-me-down grip did the trick: At sixteen, Charlie was the second-ranked junior golfer in Maryland, and the DC area's 2006 Metro Golfer of the Year. Still he wasn't among the top thousand in the national junior rankings. That's how fierce the fight has gotten in the junior ranks. Almost all of the top thousand were Sun Belt kids who played year-round, while Charlie and Tom stowed their clubs in the garage each November, beside the family car and the family golf cart.

Charlie was dying to transfer from Calverton High to the Leadbetter Academy. "I'll be able play all winter. I'll get so much better," he pleaded. Doting mom Sharon hated the idea—her baby in a boarding school! Tom fretted, too, but he could hear the hope in Charlie's golf talk. He knew how it felt to dream that golf dream.

There were benefits beyond Florida's weather and the Academy's pro-level instruction. As conservative Catholics, Tom and Sharon liked the strict rules and tight security on the IMG campus, which they hoped would delay Charlie's introduction to drinking and dating. But mainly they felt that if Charlie didn't take this chance, they might all regret it someday. Wouldn't they always wonder how good he might have gotten? They talked it out and made a family decision, with Mom reluctantly going along.

"Golf ruled our whole life when Tom was out playing pro golf," Sharon lamented. "Now it's ruling us again."

The three Winegardners flew to Florida in January 2007 and enrolled Charlie in the Academy. He started immediately—in the middle of junior year—and two months later joined the Bradenton Bunch at a tournament in Tampa. Sharon flew down from Maryland to give her baby a little pampering. "Charlie doesn't mind," she said. "If he went with the others he'd be riding a bus and staying in some crappy Super 8 Motel. This way I do the driving and we stay at the Hyatt." In fact the other Leadbetter golfers were bunked at a Courtyard by Marriott near the course that weekend, but Charlie ate better than they did—room service rather than Domino's Pizza.

Charlie was loving campus life. His favorite feature of the Academy schedule: "Only half a day of school!" And soon he got an upgrade on his dorm digs: After Sharon got a look inside his dorm—a three-bedroom, two-bath with weekly maid service that couldn't keep up with the boyish mess— she convinced her husband to pay $10,000 extra for rooms in the condo-style Academy Villas, near the baseball fields. The same strict rules applied in the Villas—no alcohol or cigarettes, no kissing or hand-holding, no leaving campus unsupervised. IMG minders, called mentors, prowled the halls, enforcing lights-out at 10 p.m. But it wasn't all discipline. Charlie and his buddy Church Waesche unwound at night watching MTV and the Golf Channel. Their condo became a favorite weekend hang for other Leadbetter golfers, and freckled Charlie became "Chuck" to his new friends, who challenged him to chipping contests in the carpeted halls: Chip a ball off the carpet into a bowl of water and win five dollars. Charlie won a few bucks off his buddies and lost a few to the school's wedge wizards.

Charlie's problem wasn't chipping. It was his long game. He was still using a baseball grip, still clouting drives that nearly reached the far end of the Leadbetter range, but losing a few left or right when his hell-bent swing let him down. "Charlie is very competitive," his instructor, Andrew Oliphant, told me, "but he needs work. He drops his right shoulder at address. His right side overpowers his swing. And he won't change that grip."

The Academy's instructors had been taught to correct even minor flaws. "That's the big difference between golf instruction now and in 1970," says Wakulsky, Leadbetter's chief of training. "In 1970, a talented junior would be told, 'Don't change a thing, kid. You can hit the ball. We don't know how you do it—it's all a mystery—but, man, don't mess with it.' Now that we have video, fitness and mental training, that talented young player is likely to be remade."

Oliphant wanted Charlie to switch to a conventional overlap or interlock grip—a move that might help his ball-striking. But Charlie's dad wasn't having it. Tom Winegardner said a grip change could throw his son off for a year. So Oliphant, who had several other students to supervise at the same time, labored to bring Charlie, baseball grip and all, more in line with the upright, efficient Leadbetter swing. Sometimes it worked, more often it didn't. Charlie's scores veered from the high 60s to the high 80s. Only a few months into the year, Tom Winegardner had his doubts about his son's scores and Oliphant's work. "I never expected David Leadbetter himself to teach Charlie, but I did expect more one-on-one attention," Tom grumbled.

Charlie was getting the standard curriculum: three to four hours of instruction each weekday, frequent IPI workouts, plus occasional rounds at El Con and occasional visits with the campus sports psychologist. The trouble, in Tom's view, was that Oliphant was supervising six students, leaving Charlie to hit balls on his own much of the time.

The Winegardners didn't complain. They didn't want to be squeaky-wheel parents, the stopwatch-wielding type who demanded special attention for their kids. But they weren't happy. "It's not as intensive as we thought it would be," Tom said. "I thought Charlie's short game, at least, would get a lot better. It hasn't. I thought they might call to ask how we think it's going, like a parent-teacher conference. They don't."

"They call to see if we want to pay extra for media training," said Sharon.

Before the tournament in Tampa, Charlie and the rest of the Bradenton Bunch were handed a 3-page *Tournament Information* flyer full of info on the Elite Jet Emerald Greens Classic (entry fee $395) and the course at Tampa's Emerald Greens Golf Club, as well as the usual bullet-point pep talk and warnings:

- **You are a guest of the golf club.**
- **You are also a representative of the David Leadbetter Golf Academy. We expect professional behavior at all times.**
- **We expect you to dress neatly. *Clothes must be ironed, shirts must be tucked in.***
- **It is simple! You are here to learn how to be a champion. So any behavior unbecoming of a superstar on the golf course will result in negative consequences.**
- **We have a _no tolerance_ policy. With any rule infraction, disciplinary action will be taken. *NO EXCEPTIONS!***
- **First time (un-PGA-tour-like conduct)—*ONE WEEK SPORT SUSPENSION***

- First time (Drinking, Tobacco, Not being where you're supposed to be, Obscenities and Unruly Behavior to General Public etc)—*TWO WEEKS GOLF SUSPENSION AND ONE MISSED EVENT*
- Second time (Drinking, Tobacco, Not being where you're supposed to be, Obscenities and Unruly Behavior to General Public etc)—*ONE MONTH GOLF SUSPENSION AND TWO MISSED EVENTS*
- Third time (Drinking, Tobacco, Not being where you're supposed to be, Obscenities and Unruly Behavior to General Public etc)—*KICKED OFF CAMPUS, SIX WEEKS SUSPENSION AND NO MORE TOURNAMENTS*

With these cautions and many swing thoughts in their heads, the golfers teed off on a sticky Saturday. Like most junior tournaments, the Emerald Greens Classic was a two-round event. It was critical to get off to a good start. A nervous Sharon Winegardner followed her son but didn't speak to him—tournament officials had warned parents not to talk to their children during play. In a sport that features a fast-growing Babel of languages, the no-talk rule is one way to keep parents from giving illegal advice during a round. But the rule can add to the atmosphere of tension at junior events. Parents keep their distance from their kids lest someone accuse them of offering advice. Kids learn to ignore their mothers and fathers. The no-talking rule leads to an odd spectacle—silent parents scurrying to hand their kids bananas or bottles of Gatorade, which the kids consume and toss over their shoulders. At today's junior-golf tournaments, many players act like princes and princesses while their parents play janitor, following along behind them, picking up bottles and banana peels.

That Saturday in Tampa, Charlie was paired with two Asian-American golfers who didn't react to their shots. He outdrove them all morning but lost ground anyway. The other two boys were discipline in motion. If a shot took a horrible bounce they nodded, reached for their golf bags and set off to make the best of a bad break. Charlie answered their calm with some all-American hollering. He was all body English, twisting in agony when a drive hooked toward trouble. From there he punched a low hook out of the woods and ran after it, Sergio Garcia–style, yelling "Go, ball!" and pumping his fist when the ball rolled onto the green.

It didn't help. He shot 87.

Trudging off the course, he was the tenth-worst golfer in a field of fifty. "I sucked. Worst golf of my life," he muttered. That 87 was likely to cost him more than self-esteem. It could cost him the ranking points he needed to qualify for bigger tournaments.

The next morning, playing early with the also-rans, Charlie lashed a couple of 310-yard drives. His body English started working. As one approach shot drifted left, he torqued his torso rightward until he nearly fell over. His ball obediently hopped to the right, toward the flag. Sharon applauded as her son fired a 71, a bright red number on the scoreboard at Emerald Greens, one of only three subpar scores all weekend. His round vaulted him all the way into the tournament's top twenty. And his stock rose. When the new rankings came out, Charlie Winegardner was the 364th-ranked junior boy golfer in the country.

Not far below Charlie in the 2007 junior rankings was one of the kids Leadbetter called "free-range golfers from the boonies." Baby-faced and wide-bodied, sporting a trucker's mesh cap and rumpled shirt, Michael Wade hadn't had ten golf lessons in his life. At seventeen, he played with mismatched clubs bought on eBay. Michael worked out in his high school weight room and teed it up in low-fee tournaments reachable in a family car that had nearly 200,000 miles on the odometer. But Michael Wade of Floyd, Virginia, population 432, figured he was lucky. He figured he had more support than a former ward of the state had any right to expect.

He was the adopted son of the Reverend Marvin Wade, pastor of the Beaver Creek Church of the Brethren, and his wife, Sandy, who worked for the county health department. The Wades adopted Michael when he was nine years old. By then he had been in Virginia's foster-care program for three years, and his youth made Sean O'Hair's look idyllic. Michael never knew his biological father. His mother was a drinker and drug abuser who used her preschooler as an accomplice in burglaries. When Michael was five, he sneaked through the window of a shuttered convenience store to help her with a heist that went wrong when he set off an alarm. His mother was arrested. Another night "she was too drunk to put the key in our door," he remembers. "She punched on the door and busted up her hand real bad. I got on my bike and rode it to a pay phone and called 911. They come down in four or five police cars, and I cried because I knew what they would do. They took my mom away and they took me away."

He was placed in a series of foster homes. One of his foster parents beat him with a wooden paddle. "This paddle had holes in it, to go through the air faster," Michael says. "He would dip you in water in the bathtub before a beating because if you were wet, it hurt more. He called them spankings, but they were beatings. You couldn't walk afterwards. You couldn't stand up."

Passed from family to family, from house to house—sometimes taken from his bed in the middle of the night—Michael lived in thirteen foster homes in three years. The only token of his former life was a Batman pillow his mother had given him. Ten years later he still slept on that pillow.

He endured every kind of abuse. "There was sexual abuse," he says. "Maybe I shouldn't say that, but it happened. I think I should tell the truth. It happened, and I hate thinking of other children it's happening to." His case came to the attention of Sandy Wade, who worked in the Montgomery County Health Department. Sandy and her husband, who had no children of their own, adopted the boy in 1999 and brought him home to Floyd County, near Roanoke, a county that has one stoplight in its 381 square miles.

Pastor Marvin Wade is a portly, silver-haired man. Outside church, he favors Bermuda shorts and a wide-brimmed white straw hat. Soon after he and Sandy adopted Michael, he took the boy to play golf at Great Oaks Country Club, which he had joined for $600. Pretty soon, Michael grew strong as a bull and began winning local junior events.

"I like to put his trophies and plaques on display," Sandy says, "but Michael takes them back and hides them in his closet. He says, 'Mom, it looks like bragging!'"

Michael Wade was the 2006 Player of the Year on the

Plantation Junior Golf Tour, a regional circuit a couple steps down from the AJGA. "He had the game for the AJGA, but that's so much entry fees and travel. We just didn't have the funds," Marvin says. The Wades tried to follow every tournament round Michael played, which was difficult when morning Sunday rounds conflicted with Pastor Marvin's often-fiery sermons. Even then they tried to catch Michael's last few holes. The instant church ended they would pile into Marvin's Chevy Impala and zip from church to the course, trusting the Lord to forgive a few extra miles per hour.

In May 2007, they drove an hour to Roanoke for Michael's biggest tournament yet. The Scott Robertson Memorial took its name from a junior golfer who died of mononucleosis in 1982. Sorrow of a later vintage hung over Virginia that chilly spring day: Only a month before, a student had shot and killed thirty-two people and himself on the Virginia Tech campus in nearby Blacksburg. Golf families driving to the course at Roanoke Country Club passed the gun shop where Seung-Hui Cho had bought his Glock 19 semiautomatic pistol.

The Scott Robertson was Michael Wade's chance to strut his stuff. Former winners included PGA Tour pros Hunter Mahan and Kevin Na, LPGA star Paula Creamer and 2006 AJGA Player of the Year Philip Francis. This year's field featured a slew of top-ranked players including more than a dozen who had flown in from the Leadbetter Academy. As he walked to the clubhouse, Michael passed two members of the Bradenton Bunch, Mu Hu and Mu's friend Tommy Chung Hao Mou. They were studying a map outside the pro shop, a map of the world dotted with stickpins showing all the players' points of origin.

"I get two pins," Mu said, touching Florida and China.

"Me too," said Tommy, touching Florida and Taiwan. The map was dotted with five pins in China, three in Japan, two in South Korea and one each in the Cayman Islands, the Czech Republic, Ecuador, England, India, Indonesia, Mexico, Poland, Scotland, Switzerland and Thailand. There were dozens scattered around the United States, with a tight cluster in Bradenton, Florida, and a lone pin representing Floyd, Virginia.

Michael dropped his eBay clubs beside the clubhouse. He was nervous, but said it was a good kind of nervous: "Ready to roll."

He came out firing pars and birdies in the first round. Pastor Marvin, walking behind him, gave the air a little punch when a putt fell in. "Atta boy." Sandy walked beside her husband, just ahead of Marvin's mother and Michael's girlfriend, Floyd County High sophomore Mandy Basham. Other than slim, smiling Mandy, the Wades were a heavyset foursome, eager to avoid long walks. Marvin trekked ahead, picking spots where they could view two holes at once. "Savin' steps," he called it. The Wades were more than a little bit country. When Michael thumped a drive that ran through a fairway, Pastor Marvin said the ball "rolled on down in the holler."

Michael knocked it from the holler to the green. As he swung, a yellow cord hanging from his pants pocket made a circle in the air. The cord was a lucky lanyard from a church camp. He wore it at school, church and on the golf course. "Even the prom," said Mandy, his prom date. At the dance, Michael had boogied with the lanyard hanging from his tux pocket. Now it swung behind him as he bombed a four-iron at the flag on a 240-yard par-three. Pastor Marvin said, "Git on!" But his son was too strong—the ball flew the green.

As Michael settled over his chip, his father said, "I'm not pulling for him to hit it close. I'm pulling for *in*." Asked if he prayed for good shots, the pastor shook his head. "Not for results," he said. "We just try to do right and earn good results." He sounded like every sports psychologist I had met who said golfers should focus on process, not outcome. "Michael's quiet about his spirituality, quieter than me. But he has good in him," Marvin went on. "He'll stick up for a kid who gets bullied at school. He knows what it's like to be at the bottom of the world."

Michael frittered away a few strokes on the back nine but held on to post a 72 that left him in sixth place, only three shots off the lead.

Meanwhile the favorite was scuffling. Mu Hu, wearing the bold orange and blue of the University of Florida Gators—the college that had won his loyalty—struck irons with such zing that one spectator gave him a wolf whistle. It's not easy living up to the nickname "One in a Billion," but Mu looked the part. His elegant swing was featured in *Golf Digest* when he was fifteen. ("He has a very dynamic golf swing, moves fluidly and, with clubhead speed of about 117 miles per hour, consistently hits the ball in the 300-yard range," Leadbetter wrote in a caption.) But Mu couldn't buy a putt today. Jenny Hu watched through Chanel sunglasses as her son, marking his ball with a Chinese coin, three-putted from four feet. "He is tired, but it's no excuse," she said. They had flown from Orlando to Charlotte to Roanoke only to be greeted with a new twist on the talking-to-kids rule: At the Scott Robertson Memorial, parents were allowed to speak to their children during play as long as they didn't give advice. With one condition: They had to speak in English.

Mu's 78 was lousy in any language. He finished the day nine shots off the lead, half a dozen shots behind the country boy in the trucker cap.

That morning, a scruffy-looking man was seen sleeping in his van in the parking lot. That man was no stalker; he was Ivan Lendl. After driving nine hours from Connecticut to meet Samantha and his three golfing daughters, who had flown up from Bradenton the day before, Lendl woke at 5 a.m. to drive thirteen-year-old Crash to the course. An hour later, he swung back to the Lendls' motel to shuttle Isabelle and Marika to their tee times, then snoozed in the parking lot for ninety minutes.

You could see the golfers' breath and practically feel the vigor of youth in them, hormones humming in their veins like juice in power lines. Their fortyish and fiftyish parents lagged behind, carrying chairbrellas and Styrofoam cups of coffee, looking tired. Lendl plopped into his folding chair under a pine tree. Being a parent was a demanding job, he said. In his view, children must learn self-sufficiency, in golf as in life. "If you do everything for them, they're just your pawn," he said. This was a page from the Earl Woods workbook. Earl never made Tiger practice or urged him to work on his game; he made Tiger *want* to practice. It was the same in the Lendl house: The girls lived to compete with Dad and each other. The Lendls debated decisions and made them together, with Ivan playing benevolent dictator. As he put it: "My word is final, except when it isn't."

A few years back, after he imposed a 9 p.m. bedtime on school nights, Marika led a mutiny, with mom Samantha's support. Faced with such fierce opposition, Ivan amended the rule: The girls could stay up later as long as their games and their grades didn't suffer.

His flexibility left him with two golfing daughters on opposite tracks in school and sport. Marika, the eldest, was headed for Vanderbilt to play college golf, while Isabelle would almost certainly turn pro when she turned eighteen. "They are different. Marika is more...social," Lendl said, making the word sound like a flaw. "Isabelle is all about her golf." There was no doubt which daughter was more like her dad.

Lendl loathes what he sees as the rampant mollycoddling of American kids. Little League trophies for everyone, just for participating? "Ridiculous!" Parents running after children, picking up their trash? "Oversupportive." He was dismayed by some of the kid-coddling he saw at the Scott Robertson: parents carrying their kids' clubs from the parking lot to the course; a Korean-American mother shadowing her daughter, holding an umbrella to protect her from the sun; another mother catching a banana peel her son tossed. "What's the matter with that boy?" Lendl asked. "He can't walk to a garbage can?"

A barking voice caught his ear. He pointed to the practice bunker. "Look there—child abuse in the sand." A fat father was spitting orders to his son, making the boy hit one explosion shot after another. The kid's technique was all wrong, but the father didn't know it. Lendl shook his head as he watched the boy swing again and again with a closed clubface, digging deep with each swing, leaving most of his shots in the bunker. "Harder!" the dad shouted. So the boy swung harder—and sent a spray of sand into his father's face.

Lendl laughed. "Serves him right!"

His daughter Marika was out of contention by then. Ivan followed her anyway, applauding a sharp iron shot that wouldn't affect the outcome. Marika would come in twenty-seventh, maintaining her ranking: tenth in the nation. Meanwhile her sister Isabelle began the final round with a chance to win the girls' division of the tournament. "We talked about how to approach that situation," Lendl said. "I told her she needed to get pumped on the first tee and stay that way. Don't wait till you've got a knife to your neck."

Isabelle reached the last hole with a one-shot lead. The 18th was a par-three, straight uphill. Her ice-gray eyes flashed as she looked up the hill. Only 154 yards long, the hole played 180. She hit a high, arrow-straight six-iron to 21 feet, then lagged to a foot and tapped in. Isabelle's ranking had slipped in recent weeks, but her second straight Scott Robertson title would boost her to third in the nation among junior girls.

Another girl impressed Ivan just as much that day. Thirteen-year-old Daniela Lendl, aka Crash, was the 285th-ranked girl in U.S. junior golf that week. Crash had earned her nickname as a tot who would run pell-mell around tennis courts until she smashed into a fence or net post. Crash had a lousy tournament, shooting 75–80–84 to finish 28 shots behind Isabelle. Yet when Ivan met her afterward, he clamped a ruddy paw on her shoulder and pulled her to him.

"You were really fighting not to make a double," he said with pride. "Good job."

"Can I get a Reese's?" Crash asked.

Candy? Her nutrition-minded father made a face, but said yes.

In the boys' bracket, Mu Hu charged into contention with one of his torrid runs of tee-to-green perfection. His front-nine 34 would have been even better if not for a trio of three-putt greens. Still, his second-round 69 gave him a chance. If Mu ever conquers his putting, the PGA Tour galleries of 2012 might sound like herds of cows, mooing his name.

Michael Wade was trying to keep up with his playing partners. One was the Leadbetter Academy's Esteban Calisto. When the two compared their lives, each found something to envy in the other: Michael, with his mismatched clubs, wished he had a gleaming, custom-fitted set like Esteban's, as well as a chance to play all winter long, while Esteban, who hadn't seen his parents in months, spotted Michael's family and girlfriend and said he was looking forward to a summer trip home to Ecuador—where he would be allowed to go out on a date. Both boys were trailing the third member of their group, a scowling Pennsylvania kid who was one of the top-ranked juniors in America. This boy muttered "shit" and "fuck" and, when a putt horseshoed around the cup, "fucking fuckit." Pastor Marvin clucked sadly at that. Michael's eyes went wide, more with amusement than shock.

The afternoon brought birdsong, the scent of flowering dogwoods and crab apple trees, warm sun slanting toward the Blue Ridge Mountains. Michael fell back, losing ground to Esteban and the blasphemer. He got a shot back at the par-three 14th, firing a five-iron that stopped an inch short of the hole. Then, gritting his teeth, he mashed a 315-yard drive at the par-five 17th, swinging so hard his mesh cap flew off. Needing eagle, he made par. He was on his way to a 24th-place finish—good enough to lift him from unlisted to 456th in the national junior boys' rankings. "I'm pretty happy," he said between bites of post-round pizza. "These other kids have had lessons all their lives. I haven't had that top-notch experience, but I'm not so far behind. I believe I can catch up."

Sean O'Hair had some catching up to do when he was Michael's age. Bullied and abused for the first nineteen years of his life, Sean broke with his hell-dad after meeting college golfer Jackie Lucas and moved in with Jackie's family in Pennsylvania. On one of their first family outings they drove to a mall, where Sean bought his first pair of blue jeans. Six months later, he married Jackie. Marc O'Hair attended the wedding but couldn't bring himself to hug Sean or wish him well.

In lieu of wedding gifts, the newlyweds asked for checks—money for minitour entry fees. They became a husband-and-wife team, with Jackie caddying for Sean on the ragtag Cleveland Tour in New England and the Gateway Tour in Florida, circuits with first-place checks of $10,000 to $15,000. Making the weekly cut paid less than $1,000. They drove from tournament to tournament in a motor home with their golden retriever, Palmer, named after Arnold Palmer. One day, the threesome was almost wiped out by a tornado in Oklahoma. While their trailer rocked and Sean and Jackie held on to doorframes, Palmer slid from wall to wall. "That was our honeymoon," Sean says with a smile. "We loved it."

Feeling fearless, he won a minitour event and then went on a tear. Sean earned $115,860 as a minor-league golfer in

2004. That fall he birdied three of the last four holes to reach the final stage of the PGA Tour's Qualifying Tournament (aka Q-School), where he finished fourth in a field of 170 pros to earn his PGA Tour card for 2005. By then Jackie's father, Steve Lucas, was Sean's caddie. After the last round of Q-School, Lucas called his daughter and handed Sean the phone. Sean couldn't speak, he was crying so hard.

At the Byron Nelson Classic in April 2005, the lanky twenty-two-year-old finished second, bringing home $670,000, enough to begin flying Jackie and their baby daughter, Molly, to Tour stops. Three months later he made his eighteenth PGA Tour start at the John Deere Classic in Illinois. On the night before the tournament he felt "weird, messed up," he says. "I was so desperate I went to a Borders store down the road and looked at a bunch of golf books." Picking up a copy of Jack Nicklaus's *Golf My Way*, he found a sketch showing Nicklaus's hip rotation. Bingo! "I'd been sliding my right hip at the start of the backswing, instead of pulling it straight back away from the ball," he said. Watching himself in a hotel mirror, he tried Nicklaus's move. "It looked right. It felt great." He shot 66 in the first round. Two more subpar rounds kept him close to the lead, and on Sunday afternoon, with his father-in-law on his bag and Jackie holding baby Molly in the crowd behind the 18th green, Sean sized up a 7-foot putt to win the tournament.

His putt, rotating smoothly end over end, fell in. Sean got a trophy, a check for $720,000 and a slathering of kisses from his girls. When he woke the next day—the morning of his twenty-third birthday—he was a winner on the PGA Tour.

Two weeks later, Marc O'Hair faxed a 17-page manifesto to the Golf Channel, the PGA Tour and the pressroom at that week's Tour event—a media trifecta that ensured blanket coverage in newspapers, magazines, radio and on TV. Among other assertions, Marc wrote:

Everyone knows that investing in a young tour player is a poor financial decision. The probability of a young player making it to the PGA Tour is less than 1%. My investment in Sean was strictly because he is my son, I love him, and no one else would have taken the financial risk . . .

I miscalculated as a rookie parent that he was going to need a period of time on his own to mature a bit more and establish his own set of principles and beliefs. He also needed to find that certain woman who would love him and fulfill his needs, perfecting you might say the "complete gladiator" . . .

I had always been fearful of the college life for Sean. The kids are worse now than when I was in college back in the 70's. Their disrespectful, hedonistic Godless attitudes along with their tattooed and pierced bodies scared the hell out of me. . . . The drinking, whoring and partying in the college life was a trap for Sean to fall into. I am a recovering alcoholic. If Sean were to begin drinking even lightly and socially, there is a high probability that he will become a drunk. Thank God he stayed away from that life, got married a virgin, and doesn't drink or smoke.

As if faxing the world about his son's virginity weren't mortifying enough, Marc went on to justify striking Sean ("There was never a slap that wasn't provoked") and defend the contract he'd made him sign ("I told him I couldn't invest his mother's and my retirement account on his game unless there would be payback later").

"And in closing," Marc concluded after "releasing" Sean from the unenforceable contract, "I would like to tell all my dear friends in the media to kiss my ass."

Asked about Sean O'Hair, Tiger Woods said, "He has as much talent as anybody out here." Sean earned $2,461,482 and the PGA Tour's Rookie of the Year award in 2005. He added $1,411,387 in 2006. With help from Jackie and her family, he had forged his own identity. There was one last adjustment to make: He had his middle name, Marc, deleted from the Tour's media guide.

On the range at the 2007 Arnold Palmer Invitational in Orlando, the six-foot-two, 165-pound O'Hair looked pencil-thin, wan and worried. "That's just how Sean looks," Jackie told me as she held their second child, two-month-old Luke. But her husband *was* worried. He was slumping again. He had made only one cut in his first six tournaments of 2007. His total earnings: $11,596. "The club's been getting stuck," he said. It's a common swing flaw: He was letting the club trail behind his body's rotation on the downswing, then using his wrists at the last instant to help the clubhead catch up.

A deliberate, even robotic swinger of the club, he stuck to a rigid pre-shot routine, even on the range. First, he poked the head of his five-iron into a pile of balls to his right. He rolled a ball into position, then took four steps back, toward the fans who leaned into the rope behind him, waving golf caps and autograph books. He peered toward his target, a yellow flag 220 yards out. He took two slow quarter-swings. He walked four steps back to the ball, spinning the club once on the second step. All this before each long, powerful swing began.

He launched a ball that sped off at a 30-degree angle, carried to the yellow flag, and fell just beyond it. He looked worried.

Leadbetter strolled past, arms crossed. He and O'Hair exchanged nods. In the past year Sean had gone to Leadbetter for private lessons, then switched from Lead to his old Academy coach Gary Gilchrist, and then turned to yet another teacher. O'Hair was practically the Leadbetter prototype: tall, strong and studious, with a head full of swing diagrams. He might return to Lead at any minute. The dance of PGA Tour golfers and their gurus found the big names changing partners from year to year and even week to week. Leadbetter had lost O'Hair, at least for now, but could pin his hopes this week on Charles Howell III or Trevor Immelman, another young pro with world-class chops. The handsome, dapper Immelman, a five-foot-nine South African with impeccable technique, was "ready to break out. Trevor is going to win, and win big," Leadbetter said.

Immelman's opposite, a lumpy, forty-six-year-old, was just now arriving on the range. While younger pros looked on, the paunchy, unshaven Mark Calcavecchia fished a ball from his own pile of range balls. His first swing produced a scalded half-shank that veered into the weeds seventy yards away. A few Tour players applauded the shot. Calcavecchia, smiling, gave a little bow. He could afford to laugh off the day's ugliest swing. The previous Sunday, he had won the PODS Championship and $954,000.

Sean O'Hair didn't notice Calcavecchia's flub. He was

back in his pre-shot routine, peering downrange as if he saw bad weather coming.

Later, O'Hair kicked off his shoes in the locker room. He nodded at the scene around him: polished wooden lockers, leather upholstery, muted flat-screen TVs tuned to MSNBC and the Golf Channel, trays of fresh cold cuts and cookies, jumbo FedEx boxes full of new clubs and clothes. "For so many years I dreamed about getting here. But now, sometimes, I forget to enjoy it," he said. "On the Tour you're always working so hard to get better—or at least not get worse." His smile was so brief you could miss it. It was the rueful smile of a Tour pro who had been missing more cuts than he made. "So I'm remembering that now—how good it is to be here. How much I love my job."

Did he think he might owe his job, at least in part, to his father? Was it possible that Marc O'Hair's plan had *worked*?

Sean shook his head. "No. I'm not here because of him. I'm here because of me. And my wife. When I met Jackie, it was like coming out of a nightmare. I saw that golf isn't war. It's a game! When you're ten or eleven years old, golf should be fun, not work." He seemed not to notice he had clenched his fist. "I mean, how could you hit a kid over a frickin' game? If you ask me, any parent who hits his kid should be thrown in jail."

Gary Gilchrist had told me: "Sean O'Hair was a great, great talent, a once-in-a-generation talent. But his father damaged him, and Sean is still dealing with that. He will always deal with that."

Confronted with that quote, Sean looked at the floor. When he spoke, his voice was soft.

"I would not disagree," he said.

Jackie said Sean had to learn how to be a grown-up. He'd been so controlled by his father that he was almost twenty before he bought that first pair of jeans, ordered his first pizza or made his first hotel reservation. But as a father, Jackie said, her twenty-four-year-old husband was a natural. His shyness vanished around Molly and Luke. Most Tour pros left their families at home while they flew from event to event, but the O'Hairs flew as a foursome. Sean couldn't bear to leave Jackie and the kids behind. He had a bag tag with Jackie's photo on it, and marked his ball with a lucky coin she'd given him.

Sean had always had talent. His minitour trials proved his grit, and teaching from Gilchrist, Leadbetter and others helped hone his technique. Now he had the support he needed to take the next step. Or, as Sean put it, "Being with Jackie and the kids, that's happiness. That's what drives me."

F I V E

Graduation: At First,
You Don't Succeed

What does it mean to learn how to win? No question means more to young golfers and their families, but the answer is elusive. Some of the most talented players bomb out at the last stage between prodigy and pro despite expert instruction and steadfast support.

In the long, screwy summer of 2007, Leadbetter found himself embroiled in one of the sports stories of the year: the ongoing meltdown of Michelle Wie. Her struggles suggested lessons both general (etiquette counts) and specific (don't try to advise B.J. Wie). They also suggested that learning how to win is like climbing a ladder: No matter how gifted you are, the best way up is one rung at a time.

In 1996, when Tiger Woods turned pro with a famous

Nike commercial ("Hello, world") and two quick Tour victories, it seemed to casual fans that he had come out of nowhere. In fact, the skinny twenty-year-old had been carefully groomed for success by parents who were ambitious, optimistic and—perhaps most important of all—patient.

Woods grew up a public-course golfer in a country-club world, a dark-skinned kid in a white man's game. But he had the consistent, unconditional love of his parents. Never doubting he was special, he learned to see trouble, whether it was racism or bumpy greens, as an affront to the natural order of the universe. As a youngster he got mad, not sad or scared, when a driving-range pro kicked him off the premises because someone complained about the "little nigger" hitting balls over the back fence.

By then he was already a junior-golf legend. The teen Tiger won the U.S. Junior Amateur three years in a row. No one else has won more than once. In 1994, the year after his third Junior Am title, he stepped up in class to the U.S. Amateur and won that, too. At eighteen, he was the youngest Amateur champion ever. Of course he won again the following year. Everyone wanted to know when he would turn pro. His father had the answer: "When he's ready."

Earl and Kultida Woods were in no hurry to capitalize on their son's talent. They wanted to let it deepen and mature. "I had one rule: Never put him in over his head," Earl told *Golf World*. "Why subject him to that? The hardest part is psychological." Rather than jump to the pro ranks before he was ready, Tiger dipped his toe into the water. Eight times. Due to his growing fame, PGA Tour sponsors lined up to offer special exemptions into their fields, and with Earl's blessing he accepted a few. Tiger teed it up in his first Tour event at age sixteen, then accepted three sponsors' exemptions into pro events at seventeen, three more at eighteen and another at nineteen. In those eight tries, the greatest prodigy in golf history made one cut.

His Amateur victories got him into the Masters, U.S. Open and British Open in 1995 and 1996. He did better in those tournaments, making four cuts in six tries, but never finished in the top 20. If Tiger's scuffling in his first pro events proves anything, it's that there is a steep learning curve between amateur phenom and pro golfer. Earl Woods recognized that fact. He insisted that his son get a firm footing at every level before stepping up to the next. It wasn't until 1996, after a third straight U.S. Amateur crown and an NCAA title at Stanford, that twenty-year-old Tiger turned pro.

Other schoolboy stars followed the same trajectory: amateur success at the national level, followed by at least a year of seasoning in college. Jack Nicklaus won two U.S. Amateurs and an NCAA title before turning pro at twenty-one. Phil Mickelson, the 1990 U.S. Amateur champion, won the 1991 Northern Telecom Open—he was the fourth amateur ever to win on Tour—and then returned to Arizona State to win the last of his three NCAA titles. Mickelson was leery of turning pro too soon. "I've got the rest of my life to beat my head against a wall playing pros," he said.

Michelle Wie was supposed to be different. She was supposed to be ready.

For starters, Michelle Wie had more talent at a younger age than any other golfer ever had, with the possible exception of Tiger. She had the grit to spend hours, weeks and months building strength in the gym, her least favorite place, until she was physically stronger than most men. She had teaching from Leadbetter and unflagging support from parents whose lives revolved around their only child.

By the time seventeen-year-old Paula Creamer gave a "kickass" speech accepting the AJGA Player of the Year award in 2005, thirteen-year-old Michelle Wie had accepted a sponsor's exemption and made a cut on the women's pro tour. Michelle was the youngest player ever to make an LPGA cut. But the willowy girl from Hawaii was just warming up. What made her world-famous was her foray into men's golf: At the 2004 Sony Open she became the fourth female—and the youngest ever—to play in a men's-tour event. Though she missed the cut by a shot, her second-round 68 amazed Arnold Palmer, who said, "She's probably going to influence golf as much as Tiger, or more."

"Give her another couple years to get stronger and she can play on the PGA Tour," said Ernie Els.

Leadbetter, who coached both players, saw an Els-like purity in Michelle's ballstriking. "The way they deliver the club to impact—with the left leg firm and the left arm and shaft in a continuous line—is perfect," he wrote in *Golf Digest*. "In the years to come, the boys may just have to watch out."

That last line carried more weight than he knew. Michelle's parents had always expected their daughter to be the best female golfer of all time. But B.J. and Bo Wie had their hearts set on something even grander than that, and so did their daughter.

"You need to remember her earliest years," Jim Loehr said. Loehr, a longtime colleague of Leadbetter's, was Michelle's sports psychologist. "What was she? A tennis kid who was so much better than all the girls that her dad said, 'You should play against the boys.' And she beat the boys, too. Later the same thing happens in golf. Match her up with a decent player, a local *star*, and she hits it eighty yards past him. The boy just wants to hide. And Michelle thinks, 'If I can do this, what *can't* women do?'"

According to one Leadbetter instructor, "Lead saw it, we all saw it: This girl wasn't just the latest junior star. This girl was *history*. Why should she spend four or five years in the AJGA, beating up on kids who were half her size and a hundred yards shorter off the tee?"

Michelle seemed destined to remake the game in her image: young, fun and "awesome," her favorite word. Her LPGA galleries quadrupled those of Annika Sorenstam, the tour's top female player. When she teed it up with the men of the PGA Tour, she overshadowed even Woods. Potential sponsors like Nike and Sony wanted to make the Wies rich the moment she turned pro—a fact that preoccupied her father, who was spending about $70,000 a year on her expenses, too much for a college professor to afford for long. Still B.J. insisted he was in no hurry. In 2004, when Michelle was fourteen, he told the *Honolulu Advertiser* she wouldn't turn pro until she was eighteen. In fact, he said, she might wait till she was twenty-two. "Eighteen is too young to play professional golf," he said. "She can really burn out at eighteen if she turns professional."

Like other golf dads, B.J. called Earl Woods his role model. He had papered Michelle's room with posters of Tiger when she was little. He kept swing-sequence photos of

Tiger in his wallet, to compare them with Michelle's swing while she played. But Earl Woods never hovered over his child the way B.J. Wie did. Earl didn't caddie for his kid as B.J. did—most notoriously at the 2003 U.S. Women's Open at Pumpkin Ridge Golf Club in Oregon, where the inexperienced Wies trampled pro-golf etiquette. B.J. walked when other players were hitting; he let Michelle hit out of turn and didn't notice when she stepped on playing partner Danielle Ammaccapane's putting line. After the round Ammaccapane, thirty-seven, told Michelle off. "You're the worst kid I've even seen play golf. You'll never make it to the LPGA," she shouted. B.J. claimed Ammaccapane shoved Michelle (a charge he soon retracted), and Michelle went on to finish thirty-ninth with Gilchrist carrying her bag. After that, B.J. admitted his micromanaging wasn't helping his daughter. "Maybe it's time to let her go," he said.

But B.J. was not the kind of parent who lets his daughter go. I saw that myself when I arranged a round of golf for Michelle and Donald Trump.

Both golfers were larger than life—the six-foot teenager famous for her 300-yard drives and the blustery billionaire whose reality program, *The Apprentice*, was the number-one show on TV. One night in Orlando in 2004, after Michelle spent the day tuning her swing with Leadbetter, I took her and her parents out for sushi. Michelle yawned and rolled her eyes while her father discussed his plans for her career. She brightened when the talk turned to Tiger ("He's so great") and Adam Scott ("He's so cute"). When I mentioned that Trump was a golfer, she said that playing with him would be awesome.

True enough. Trump had a lusty swing and a colorfully foul vocabulary. He was grand company on the golf course. One of the perks of playing his courses with him—he owned half a dozen—was that you never had to wait: A minion rode ahead in a golf cart, telling players, "Step aside, mister. Trump's coming through." You could play eighteen holes in two and a half hours. During one round at Trump National, his course in Westchester County, New York, a video crew from *The Apprentice* filmed us. At the 13th hole, a long par-three over a pond to a green at the foot of a 100-foot waterfall, Trump hit his tee shot into the pond. He reloaded, knocked another one into the pond, then teed up a third ball and knocked it on the green. "And *that*," he said, "is reality TV." When the segment aired, viewers saw only the good shot.

When I mentioned that Michelle Wie wanted to meet him, Trump said, "Great! We'll play here. My treat." Michelle had a trip to New York coming up. Trump planned a round for the two of them at Trump National. Then B.J. Wie got involved. He phoned Trump's secretary to say he expected The Donald to pay travel expenses—not just for Michelle but for her parents, too. This would have sounded familiar to USGA officials who'd had to deal with B.J.'s demands. Next came another call: Now B.J. wanted his family put up *gratis* in a Trump hotel.

I heard from an angry Trump. "This guy!" he said. "He's out of line."

The round was canceled. Michelle missed her chance to out-drive The Donald. Trump had offered hospitality; B.J. responded with greed.

Michelle's father was still calling the shots a year later, when she finished second to Sorenstam in the 2005 LPGA Championship, pounding drives forty yards past Annika's. For all his talk about Earl Woods, B.J. encouraged his daughter to bypass the step-by-step ascent that had prepared Tiger for professional combat. Michelle had won no U.S. Juniors, no U.S. Amateurs. Still the drumbeat grew: When would she turn pro?

There had been a super-size controversy that week: When the LPGA balked at making Michelle the first amateur ever invited to play in the event, tournament sponsor McDonald's threatened to pull out. The LPGA caved, leaving other players grumbling. A few weeks later, Michelle held the third-round lead at the U.S. Women's Open before stumbling to an ugly 82 on Sunday. Morgan Pressel, a teen star who had come up through junior and amateur golf, thought she knew why. "Michelle hasn't played a lot of junior golf, so she hasn't learned how to finish tournaments," she told *Sports Illustrated*. But that 82 at the Open looked like a fluke when Michelle tied for second at the Evian Masters and third at the Women's British Open. No other teen had ever played so well in the women's majors. Had she not been an amateur, she would have earned more than $500,000 in those four events alone. That last detail made a strong impression on B.J. Wie.

Another way to read the numbers can be found in a detail that went unreported. At one of the LPGA majors Michelle played as an amateur, she came to the final hole, a reachable par-five, with a chance to win. "Hit driver," said her caddie. "Then you can hit a seven-iron on the green, make the putt and *win*."

"No," she said, handing back the driver. "My dad wants me to hit five-wood." Rather than playing to win, she was playing it safe. By protecting her spot in the top ten, she could enhance her chances of getting into other majors.

On October 5, 2005, B.J. Wie called a press conference at the Kahala Mandarin Oriental Hotel in Honolulu. Michelle dressed up for her coming-out party in spike heels that added two inches to her six-foot-one stature and a hot-pink blouse with the Nike swoosh over her heart. Giggling, she announced that she was turning pro. "I'm so excited!" she gushed. B.J. had arranged endorsement deals with Nike, Sony and other sponsors for around $20 million a year, assuring that Michelle would be the best-paid female golfer in history before she struck a shot as a pro. Asked why she should be worth so much, she said, "I don't know. But I'm going to try hard to live up to it. I know I have to win."

Later, B.J. burbled about leading his daughter to the press conference: "When I was bringing her downstairs, it felt like a wedding." Like a bride, his daughter would have "new responsibilities," he said. "She has to be able to handle much higher expectations."

Michelle's first act as a professional was to donate $500,000 to victims of Hurricane Katrina in New Orleans. The donation was her idea—the kindness of a happy, newly wealthy girl with a sunny future. Six days later, Michelle Wie turned sixteen.

All this had happened before. Back in 2001, another Leadbetter prodigy made headlines.

Like Tiger Woods, Sean O'Hair and Michelle Wie, Ty

Tryon had a golfing father who just *knew* his kid was going to be a star. William Augustus Tryon III, a North Carolina mortgage banker, named his son William Augustus IV but called him Ty after the golf pro in *Caddyshack*. Bill Tryon was far richer than Earl Woods or B.J. Wie, so he built his son a tyke-size course on the family estate near Raleigh. The boy was winning junior tournaments before he reached the second grade. Soon the Tryons moved to Florida so Ty could attend the Leadbetter Academy, where his work ethic made an instant impression.

"Ty was golden, Ty was brave," says Gilchrist. Ty would jog from the range to the gym, where he often worked out so hard that he threw up. He made up for lost calories by wolfing down burritos and protein shakes, then jogged back to the range to challenge his buddy O'Hair, who was two years older, to a driving or chipping contest. Their fathers stood nearby, eagle-eyeing every practice session. Ty sometimes joked with his dad or lipped off to him. There was none of that between Sean and Marc O'Hair. Ty, a freer spirit, noticed that his friend didn't smile much.

Like Sean, Ty grew fast once he hit his mid-teens, sprouting from five foot six and 130 pounds to five foot eleven and 170, adding strength and leverage to his Leadbetter swing. Suddenly, he was Tiger-long. As a high school sophomore he Monday-qualified for the PGA Tour's Honda Classic and was paired with Tour veteran Tom Lehman. "This skinny kid steps up on the first tee and hits his drive 320 down the middle," Lehman recalls. "I'm thinking, 'Holy smokes!'" All day the sixteen-year-old outdrove the forty-two-year-old who had won the British Open and been number one in the world, while calling him Mr. Lehman.

"You're making me feel old," Lehman said. "Call me Tom."

"OK, Mr. Lehman."

Ty finished thirty-ninth that week. He would have won $12,000 had he not been an amateur. Four months later, he fired a first-round 65 to grab the lead in the 2001 B.C. Open. That round stamped a footnote in the record books. Question: How many players Ty's age ever led a PGA Tour event? Answer: One—him.

Ty left the Academy in the middle of his sophomore year and began taking private lessons from Leadbetter in Orlando. Back in Bradenton, Gilchrist wasn't pleased. "Kids need other kids," he said. Gilchrist believed in peer pressure as well as technique. He thought the best way to nurture golf prodigies was to keep them surrounded by others their own age. Ty was now literally peerless—living at home with his parents, working one-on-one with Lead, outdriving his elders on the range, shooting 65s in practice rounds. That summer his father began asking golf insiders what Ty might be worth as a pro.

Why wait? Ty wouldn't be going to college. He was one of the least motivated high school students since Andre Agassi, another Bradenton-trained phenom who never cracked a book. Ty was going to be movie-star handsome once his acne cleared up, and his power game would be catnip to sponsors and fans. After growing into his Lead-programmed swing, he was driving the ball out of sight—"Nuked it!" he liked to say. He was deft with his wedges, which he could fly in high with toothy backspin or bump to the green like a Scottish linksman. And so in the pre-9/11 summer of 2001, Ty Tryon turned pro. He was seventeen.

"He has my backing," Leadbetter told the press. "Sure,

there will be naysayers, but it's been done in other sports. Kids are much more advanced in training, skills and fitness than ever before."

Gilchrist kept his doubts to himself.

And Ty made Lead look like a prophet at Q-School that December, when the kid with the perfect Leadbetter swing made history.

The date was December 3, 2001. A thousand miles to the north, the World Trade Center lay in ruins, the rubble still burning under the surface. Ty had watched on TV as the towers fell. But life went on and so did golf, and now the top phenom since Tiger was at Bear Lakes Country Club in West Palm Beach for the sixth and final round of the PGA Tour's Q-School, the game's cruelest challenge. Each year at Q-School, hundreds of talented pros vie for a few spots on the PGA Tour, where one good week can be worth $1 million and a good year can set your family up for life. At Q-School the pressure ratchets upward for a grueling, gut-wrenching week until, on the last day, veteran pros slip into the bushes to vomit before teeing off.

Not Ty. He was a kid on a hot streak, not an old pro fighting to keep his career alive. He thought Q-School was fun. On the last day of Q-School in 2001, he belted a 300-yard drive down the heart of the first fairway, flipped a wedge shot to six feet and knocked in the putt. One under. An hour later, he birdied the 7th and 8th holes. Three under.

This was not supposed to happen. Three months of sectional and regional qualifying had culled any pretenders from thousands of entrants, leaving 140 survivors to duke it out at Bear Lakes. Only 35 would win PGA Tour cards entitling them to tee it up in 2002 with Tiger, Phil and golf's other multimillionaires. A Tour card was so precious that it wasn't really a card at all—the Tour's official ID was a gold money clip emblazoned with the player's name.

That morning, with five rounds in the books and one to play, Ty looked to be out of the money, three shots out the top 35. He'd have to shoot 67, maybe even 66—a career round—to make up three shots on this field of professionals.

At the par-five ninth the teenager lashed a 227-yard three-iron to the green and sank a ten-foot putt for eagle. Five under. At the 15th, another par-five, his two-iron from 240 yards bit the green ten steps behind the flag. Two-putt birdie. At the 18th, where another player got so pumped that he hit his eight-iron approach over the green and the crowd onto the clubhouse roof, Ty tapped in as if he spent most Mondays making history instead of taking it in high school. He had done the ridiculous—shot 66 in the final round of Q-School. Suddenly Ty was international news, the youngest player ever to earn a PGA Tour card. Coming off the course with news photographers and a Golf Channel camera chasing him, he got a hug from his dad. He gave the crowd a wave and a shy smile. His future was as golden as the sun over West Palm Beach.

Ty's Q-School heroics earned him PGA Tour membership and $25,000. That night the Tryons went out to celebrate. The hero was still underage, so his dad ordered a round of Shirley Temples. Ty's father had arranged for him to be represented by IMG, and now the boy's IMG agent seized the moment, signing more than $2 million in sponsorship deals with Callaway, FootJoy and Target. Within weeks, Ty was bombing around Orlando in his dream vehicle, a glitter-blue Cadillac Escalade with stereo speakers that could drown out a jet. The SUV cost $55,000, the sound system another $30,000.

His parents, agent and coaches, including Leadbetter—collectively called Team Ty—had seen flashes of brilliance from him. Maybe they mistook those flashes for the steady fire a Tour pro needs. If so, they weren't the only ones. He was such a crowd pleaser that another Tour rookie, Pat Perez, griped about playing with him. Fans cheered Ty's pars, said Perez, "then I make birdie and you can hear the wind blow." But after his grand day at Q-School, Ty sputtered.

First he came down with mononucleosis, a teenager's malady seldom seen on Tour. Then he had to have his tonsils out. The side effects of a prescription acne remedy blurred his vision, gave him nosebleeds and sapped his strength. On some days his drives carried 230 yards instead of 280. He had barely started, but golf on Tour was becoming a chore.

He could have used a friend among the older pros, but he annoyed them with juvenile antics. Ty would show up only minutes before his tee time, fumbling in his bag for a ball or a tee. After a bit of his old brilliance he'd go bogey-double-double, shrugging off lousy shots as if he didn't care. He skipped lessons with Lead, pleading illness, only to be seen driving around Orlando with his high school buddies.

"Ty has a lot to learn," Leadbetter told me at the time. "But he's going to be around for a long time, and he is going to be a star."

Yet the teen sensation made only one cut in his rookie year. He would have lost his Tour card if not for a medical exemption the Tour granted after his bout with mono. The next year, 2003, he finished tenth at Bay Hill, his home course, to win $93,375. That spurred another family celebration, but it was short-lived. At Pebble Beach that same month, he missed the cut by fifteen strokes, spraying drives and gagging short putts. Driving into the players' parking lot at PGA Tour events, he had to fight the urge to escape—to spin his Escalade around and peel out to Anywhere But Here. Looking lost, he went on to miss seventeen cuts in twenty-one tries. The top 125 players on the money list keep their cards every year; his $125,878 left him 195th on the list, bouncing him off the Tour.

"Ty lacked toughness," former Leadbetter lieutenant Mitchell Spearman says. "He had a beautiful swing, but that's not enough. At the professional level, you're going to take it on the chin again and again. You need the resilience of a boxer, and that's *learned*. It takes years." Spearman accepts the conventional view of a young pro's apprenticeship: two years on the minor-league Nationwide Tour and two on the PGA Tour. Without that battle experience, "You get on a bad run and think, 'Maybe I'm not ready.' And in this game, self-doubt is poison."

The best junior golfers haven't tasted that poison. All they've done is dominate. They may seem as calm and confident as Tiger Woods or Annika Sorenstam, and may even *feel* that way, but their confidence is untested. It is a form of innocence.

Mickelson didn't win for a year and a half after he turned pro. He spent another decade knocking on the door at the majors before he broke through at the 2004 Masters. Nick Price thinks four to eight years is a reasonable time for a pro to learn his trade. "It took me ten years," says Price. "But the process is usually the same: First you start making cuts. You get a few top 30s and then top 10s. One day you're in position to win. You fail. You might fail six or seven or ten times, but that's OK. Because you don't learn to win by winning. You learn to win by *being in the mix down the stretch*. Learning to breathe in that atmosphere."

Ty would tell me later that turning pro was a "family decision," but he was only seventeen at the time. He wanted to buy an SUV with a "smokin' sound system," and he got his wish. But the price turned out to be higher than the $85,000 he paid for his candy-blue Escalade. It was higher than he could have known. Too precocious for his own good, he had made even Leadbetter believe he was so gifted he could skip the learning process that takes older pros years to complete. So rather than work his way through the amateur ranks to an apprenticeship on the Nationwide Tour, followed by four or more years of notching the occasional PGA Tour top 10 and getting into the mix down the stretch—rather than learning his trade—Ty had one pass-fail year to prove himself.

He failed. After flunking off the big tour in 2003, Ty got a quick look at the Nationwide Tour on his way down. He nuked the ball an average of 299 yards in Nationwide events in 2004, but his drives bounced into so many dark corners that golf's Icarus earned only $9,058 all year. And with that, he fell out of sight.

The more the game progresses, the smarter Earl Woods looks. Even Leadbetter now admits that Ty should have moved up the way Tiger did, testing himself at every stage, proving himself to himself until he knew he belonged at the game's highest level. As Leadbetter learned in his years with Nick Faldo, Greg Norman, Ernie Els and other pros, the smallest swing flaw tends to worsen under pressure. The smallest kernel of self-doubt turns the mind to popcorn under pressure. That's why you need more than a great swing to survive on tour—you need a resilient swing and a psyche to match. Ty had neither.

The stakes were even higher with Michelle Wie. She had a chance to be the greatest female athlete in sports history. Her role model was Tiger, not Annika. When she first met Gilchrist she said, "I want to win the Masters." Given Ty's misfortunes, it should have been clear that such a prospect should be handled with care. Once-in-a-generation talent could be a fragile commodity. Even Michelle might be subject to the malady that strikes players who get out of their depth, the golfer's version of the bends. But Team Wie figured it could train her better than Earl Woods had trained Tiger, or at least faster.

Why did Leadbetter go along? Did he want to make up for being wrong about Ty? Did he want to outshine Butch Harmon and Hank Haney, his golf-guru rivals? Or did he really think Michelle should turn pro at fifteen?

The answer: None of the above. It wasn't Leadbetter's call.

"Lead was on the team, but B.J. *was* the team," a source close to the Wies says. "B.J. knew he had an incredible, historic talent under his thumb, and he used that leverage to gain access to some of the top people in the game. But here's the thing about B.J. Wie: He solicits advice from everybody and takes advice from nobody."

Two weeks after Michelle stepped into the professional ranks, she made her pro debut at the LPGA's Samsung World Championships in Palm Desert, California as the most talked-about rookie since Tiger Woods came in fourth to earn $53,126. Or so she thought. After she finished, *Sports Illustrated* writer Michael Bamberger told tournament officials he had seen Michelle take what looked like an illegal drop. They led the surprised, worried teen back to the spot where she'd taken a drop after hitting into a bush, and determined that she had dropped the ball twelve to fifteen inches too close to the green. This was worse than a rookie mistake: She had broken the Rules of Golf. Michelle was disqualified. While writer Bamberger caught heat for his "participatory journalism," Michelle lost the first paycheck of her career. She left the course empty-handed.

"I don't feel like I cheated," she told reporters, fighting tears.

The money didn't matter. The Wies were rolling in sponsors' dollars. But getting DQ'd from her first pro event shook Michelle. She missed cuts in two men's tournaments before earning her first paycheck at the LPGA's Fields Open, coming in third to win $72,875. More dazzling was the diamond-studded Omega watch she received before the final round. Omega was paying the Wies about $2 million a year to be one of her sponsors, but to Michelle 2,000,000 was a number on a spreadsheet. The watch thrilled her more. "It's sparkly!" she said. "I kept checking the time, like, every five minutes."

Playing against men in the SK Telecom Open in South Korea, she made the cut while ten-deep galleries chanted "*On-ni*," Korean for "big sister." Her thirty-fifth-place finish paid $4,303. It sounded like a moral victory until a bigger number leaked out. Before the tournament, B.J. had agreed to an appearance fee for Michelle. Such fees are banned in the U.S. but legal on the Asian Tour. Her fee was $700,000—for an event with a total purse of $600,000. Thailand's Prom "Big Dolphin" Meesawat got $127,523 for winning the tournament.

Also in the field that week was Ty Tryon, five years into his pro career, bouncing around the world looking for a tour to play on. Twenty-one-year-old Ty missed the cut by a dozen shots.

Sixteen-year-old Michelle showed her potential in the first three women's majors of 2006, finishing third, fifth and third again. She was "in the mix" now, as Nick Price puts it, but was mixed up, too, constantly stumbling over the unwritten rules of professional conduct. Her obsession with making history by playing male pros hadn't endeared her to LPGA colleagues who figured, correctly, that Michelle saw women's golf as a minor league by comparison. Her on-course manners didn't help, either. She would finish eighteen holes without speaking to her playing partner. And while all the other pros, even the rookies, knew to shake hands with each other and with the scorekeeper at the end of a round, and to thank the volunteer who'd carried the sign showing their scores, Michelle would blow past them all, ignoring everyone but her dad. She was unprofessional at best—untutored by a father who knew less about pro etiquette than she did—and arrogant at worst.

"Either way, her behavior is not right," says Steve Elling, then of the *Orlando Sentinel*. "The other players resent her, and she deserves it."

Her caddies could have helped. Some tried, but not for long. Team Wie fired ten caddies by the end of her first year as a pro, often leaving B.J. to carry his daughter's bag yet again.

Michelle was still the public's favorite female golfer. She was still a media darling. In May 2006, she was named one of *Time* magazine's "100 People Who Shape Our World," along with President George Bush, Hillary Clinton, Bill Gates and the pope. Tiger Woods didn't make the list. At the Women's World Match Play Championship she faced Brittany Lincicome, a young, self-taught Floridian with a flying ponytail and crowd-pleasing power of her own. While the players ignored each other, the behavior of a pair of gallery members spoke volumes. When Brittany outdrove Michelle, Brittany's father was seen high-fiving Paul Creamer, Paula's father. When Brittany won a hole on her way to knocking Michelle out of the tournament, the two dads bumped chests like football stars after a touchdown.

Being loathed by tour insiders took a toll on Michelle. According to Loehr, the sports psychologist who began seeing her in 2004, she would go from the course to her hotel room, shut the door and cry. Like Ty, she was making blunders that irked other pros already primed to resent her for her easy ascent, her sponsors' exemptions, her diamond watch and instant millions—blunders she wouldn't have made had she risen through the amateur ranks and the minor-league Futures Tour, learning the unwritten rules along the way. For a teenager the psychologist calls "an open, big-hearted girl," the hostility she faced on tour was toxic. She felt friendless— no way to feel when you're hitting a ball over water to a tucked pin on national TV.

Nine months after her pro debut, Michelle Wie's career was imploding. At the 2006 John Deere Classic in July, playing on yet another sponsor's exemption against male pros, she was out of contention—ten shots off the projected cut—when she collapsed with heat exhaustion. It was an odd swoon for one of the fittest female golfers ever, a strong six-footer who pumped iron and ran on a treadmill forty-five minutes a day, five days a week. A month later, at the Women's British Open, she grounded her club in a bunker—a two-stroke penalty. "I guess I knew the rule wrong," she explained lamely. B.J. fired her caddie.

On it went: Teeing it up against men in the Omega European Masters, she finished last, missing the cut by fourteen strokes. Trying again against men in the PGA Tour's 84 Lumber Classic, she missed the cut by thirteen. Young LPGA golfers like Paula Creamer, Brittany Lincicome and Morgan Pressel, not to mention a few thousand unknown male pros, could have done better. But they weren't invited. Sponsors of men's and women's events kept inviting Michelle because she sold tickets like Hannah Montana. She might be winless in thirty-three LPGA tournaments including nine as a pro, but Michelle wasn't just the biggest star in women's golf. Along with Woods and Phil Mickelson, she was one of the three biggest stars in golf.

In October, on her way to a seventeenth-place finish in the LPGA's twenty-player Samsung World Championships, she tweaked her right wrist while hitting a shot off a cartpath. In November she finished second-to-last in another men's event, shooting 81–80 to miss the cut by seventeen strokes. "I'm looking forward to going home and working on my swing with David Leadbetter," she told Japanese reporters. "I want to play a lot of men's events next year."

Nick Faldo shook his head when he heard that. Now a

TV commentator (with his own golf school on the side), Faldo thought Michelle was being mismanaged. "If she went to Q-School and got her card, I'd say, 'Good on you, girl,'" he told me. "But these sponsors' exemptions are wearing a bit thin. I'd advise her to dominate the LPGA before playing the men."

Leadbetter urged the Wies not to accept a sponsors' invitation to the PGA Tour's Sony Open in January 2007. They ignored his advice. Playing with her injured wrist wrapped in surgical tape, Michelle teed up against Vijay Singh, Jim Furyk and 140 other Tour pros. She missed the cut by fourteen shots. "I have a lot of game, it's just not showing right now," she said. Columnist Mike Lupica of the New York *Daily News* jeered that she had missed the cut "by two touchdowns."

It didn't help that another Hawaiian teen set the golf world on its ear in the same event. Tadd Fujikawa, three months younger than Michelle and a foot shorter, played with a driver that went up to his Adam's apple. The five-foot-one teenager was only fourteenth in the boys' junior rankings, well behind Peter Uihlein and Bank Vongvanij and a few slots above Mu Hu. Yet he made the Sony cut and went on to finish twentieth. Sixteen-year-old Fujikawa, a high school sophomore, was the youngest to make a PGA Tour cut in fifty years (bumping Ty Tryon from the record book). Asked when he would turn professional, he said, "After high school. I'm not turning pro before high school is over. No way." That gave him two and a half years to prepare, and maybe grow to five foot two.

Around this time, Michelle was thinking about college. She had long dreamed of going to Stanford, Tiger's old

school, even though she had given up any chance to play college golf by turning pro. On a campus visit after the Sony
Open, the richest Stanford recruit went jogging with the
women's golf team. She tripped and fell, breaking her left
wrist. Now she had one wrist taped and the other in a cast.
The injury gave her a two-month break.

"Why do people hate me? Why are they so hard on me?"
she asked her sports psychologist. She meant reporters like
Golf Digest's Jaime Diaz, who called her miseries "one of the
biggest meltdowns ever by a teenage sports prodigy."

It was fair to ask if the people who were "so hard on me"
might also include Michelle's parents. By now her psyche was
as fragile as her wrists. In fact, Loehr believed his client's latest injury may not have been wholly accidental. As he put it,
"Sometimes athletes get injured to escape an impossible situation." Did Michelle want to get hurt, at least subconsciously?
Was she that unhappy with the turn her life had taken? There
were no answers from the Wies, who had frozen out all outsiders. As Diaz wrote, "Camp Wie is sealed tight, determined
that no human frailty be revealed."

Some of the family's advisers couldn't hide their dismay.
They wanted to vent. "We're feeding a monster. All of us,"
one said. This person hated seeing Michelle run ragged—
flying around the world to meet tournament and corporate
commitments, playing male pros, pushing to play when she
was hurt—despite warnings from trusted advisers that her
future was at risk. "I'm disgusted by what her parents and
agents did to Michelle. They sold her. For $10 million up-
front, they *sold* the best female talent the game ever had."

Michelle returned to competition in May 2007 at the

LPGA's Ginn Tribute. She committed another gaffe before play began. LPGA pros aren't allowed to practice on the host course late in the week before a tournament, but there she was, knocking balls around RiverTowne Country Club in Mount Pleasant, South Carolina. It wasn't technically illegal because she was not an LPGA member, but she seemed to be seeking an unfair advantage. Her parents and her manager, Greg Nared, should have known better. A delegation of LPGA players marched into a meeting with tour officials to complain about the Wies' rule-bending.

At the Ginn Tribute, Michelle strode to the tee with a bandage around her right wrist. She wore a yellow Nike blouse and white Nike cap. Sponsorship deals mandated the Nike swoosh over her head and heart, as well as the Oreo-size Omega watch on her left wrist. An hour into her first round, a dreadful shot left her an unplayable lie. "Go back to the tee," B.J. said. He should have known better. Parents aren't allowed to give advice. Michelle's playing partners called him on it, but a rules official gave B.J. a pass, saying Michelle had not asked for his help. That call saved her a two-stroke penalty. But two strokes were a traffic ticket compared to the train wreck that was coming.

On her 12th hole, a par-five, Michelle wound up and cranked a drive that soared over gallery, trees and out-of-bounds stakes, over a sidewalk to a parked car sixty yards from the nearest fairway. Her ball bonked off the car, hopped back toward the course and rolled toward a storm drain. If ever a shot exemplified a player's year, this was the one. Down the drain it went. Michelle, looking stricken, teed up another ball and hooked it into a swamp. By the time she putted out, she had made a 10 on the hole. Before she knew it she was 14 over par for the day, and now another rule came into play: Rule 88.

In what some LPGA pros saw as a delicious irony, Rule 88 applied to nonmembers playing on sponsors' exemptions. Those who shot 88 or worse would be banned from LPGA events for the rest of the year. Fourteen over par with two holes to play, Michelle was on the brink. Two more bogeys would ruin her year. She would be stuck at home while Sorenstam, Lorena Ochoa, Morgan Pressel and Brittany Lincicome made money and headlines.

Now came a scene unprecedented in LPGA history. Manager Nared conferred with a tour official. Minutes later, Michelle quit. "We're not going to play anymore," she announced. Team Wie zipped off to the clubhouse in a golf-cart caravan, with B.J. in the lead cart and Nared perched on the back of another, hanging on.

At a press conference, speaking in clipped sentences that sounded coached, Michelle said, "I don't think about shooting 88. That's not what I do." Why had she quit? "I had issues with my wrist." Yet she hadn't winced or shown any other signs of distress. And within forty-eight hours, she was pounding balls on the driving range again.

That was too much for Ginn Tribute host Sorenstam to stomach. Michelle's behavior showed "a lack of respect and class," she told reporters.

"I don't think I have to apologize for anything," Michelle shot back. As for complaints that she'd been chilly to pro-am partners, she said, "Somebody made a false accusation."

Team Wie's relations with the tour were fraying fast. As

LPGA commissioner Carolyn Bivens dryly put it, "Those who are advising her, I have to hope, are keeping her best interests in mind."

At the center of the storm stood Leadbetter, a bony lightning rod. Reporters were calling his star pupil's year a disaster. *Golf Digest's* Diaz described Michelle as "trapped and unhappy and alienated." According to sportswriter Elling, "She needs to stop. Just stop." Others called B.J. Wie the worst golf dad in the game. Gary Gilchrist, who had left Leadbetter to run a rival academy, said privately that B.J. was a threat to Michelle's career. But when Gilchrist went public, he ripped Lead.

"They keep persisting with David," he said of the Wies, "and it's not working. Her tempo is gone. She's dropping the club to the inside too much, and snap-hooking and blocking the driver."

In the quiet of his office at ChampionsGate, Leadbetter's frustration showed. He had been in a dodgy position for months. He had urged B.J. Wie not to rush Michelle back from her injuries, but B.J. ignored his advice. And B.J. was still in charge. Lead might be the most famous guru in the game, but he was still an employee. If he argued too much, B.J. could fire him and take his daughter back to Gilchrist, or hand her over to Butch Harmon or Hank Haney. The plain commercial fact of the matter was that losing Michelle would damage the Leadbetter franchise. More important to Lead was that he believed he was the right coach for Michelle. He admitted that her quest to play the men's tour had backfired, but thought she could still be the best female golfer of all time.

"I still maintain that Michelle has the potential to play

with the men," he said, sitting in the dim indoor light he preferred. "Right now, though, she should be proving herself against the women. Playing week in and week out on the LPGA, she could win eight or nine times a year." That would be a tall order for a young woman who had yet to win as a pro. And it wasn't an option in any case: "She is contracted to play certain tournaments, and that's *part of her appeal—*playing against the men," Lead said. "These are family decisions."

There was the rub. Wie family decisions had long since acquired a corporate dimension, since Michelle's sponsors weren't paying $20 million a year for the next Paula Creamer. They wanted the female Tiger Woods. A Tigress.

"When Michelle was fifteen or sixteen, she would start her swing thinking, 'I can conquer the world.' Now her mindset is totally different," said Leadbetter. At seventeen, her swing thoughts included the fear of shooting 88, the fear of embarrassing her parents and her sponsors, the fear of becoming a higher-profile, female version of Ty Tryon. A Tygress.

If Tiger Woods was the engine driving golf's recent growth, Ty Tryon was roadkill. I found him beside a cartpath at Martin Downs Country Club in Palm City, Florida, only fifteen miles from the scene of his Q-School triumph six years before. He looked tired. He had grown a thick, dark Abraham Lincoln beard. He was twenty-two years old.

Ty socked a five-iron, his long, upright swing delivering clubface to ball with a loud *clack!* He finished with his hands high, holding the pose—the classic Leadbetter follow-through. The ball carried 212 yards, rocketing over the tree line, zeroing in on the flag as it fell. It bounced and one-hopped the flagstick.

An ace? Almost. His ball was in yummyland—Tour talk for a tap-in.

Nobody applauded. Ty's gallery at this minitour event, officially named Tournament #5 in the Gateway Tour's 2007 spring series, consisted of squirrels and a crow. The Gateway Tour, a third-tier circuit, was a form of legal gambling. Each week, players paid about $1,000 apiece to compete for a prize pool of about $80,000. A victory paid $12,000 or so, while making the cut meant earning about $100 after expenses. Chucking his five-iron into the black Tour bag strapped to his golf cart, Ty hopped in and motored toward the green. There were no caddies on the Gateway Tour. "It's weird, driving a cart," he said, "but I'm not complaining. As long as I make a few cuts, I've got a place to play."

As a rising star of seventeen, he had looked younger than his age. Now twenty-two, he could pass for thirty. His look was Golf Goth: black shoes, black knee-length shorts, black Under Armour shirt, wraparound sunglasses, black Callaway cap. The biggest surprise was the beard covering the scars left by his adolescent acne.

The teen Ty, whose Q-School exploits landed him on the front page of *USA Today*, was hailed as the next Tiger Woods. But he'd had only one golden day on the course since then. After falling off the PGA Tour and the Nationwide Tour, he had hacked his way through golf's wilderness to the Hooters Tour. A notch above regional minitour events, Hooters tournaments at least paid more than a week's expenses if you made the cut, and at a 2005 Hooters event in Clermont, Florida, Ty did more than make the cut. He made a late birdie to tie for the final-round lead. Just then, as if to spite him, a blanket of fog rolled in off a nearby swamp. The fog was so thick that play had to be stopped. Ty waited out the fog delay in his Escalade—the one with the killer sound system, one of the last reminders of his days as the next Tiger. He tried to nap. It didn't work. Finally, after two hours, the sun burst through the fog. Ty tried to keep his breathing steady as he stuck a tee in the ground at the 15th hole. He torqued his torso as far as it would go, then fired the muscles of his core, pulling the clubhead through its long arc to the ball, which rocketed toward a thick stand of palm trees in the distance. Toward trouble.

For once Ty's ball did him a favor. It hopped and stopped in the fairway. He birdied two of the closing four holes to win by three strokes. Four long years after Q-School, Ty Tryon had won a professional event.

He was thrilled. But at the same time he wasn't. He knew his $11,000 first-place check wasn't caddie money on the big Tour, where Phil Mickelson's victory that week paid nearly $1 million. While Mickelson answered questions at a PGA Tour press conference, Ty spoke to a couple of local reporters. "What am I supposed to do, jump in the air?" he asked them, sounding testy. "I just played the way I can if I don't shoot myself in the foot."

Four years later, that Hooters victory remained the lone highlight of Ty's post-PGA Tour career. With no playing privileges on any circuit, he had knocked around Europe, North Africa and Asia, earning an occasional short stack of some currency he barely recognized. He was still a magician around the green on his good days. He was still Tiger-long. But unlike Woods, the sport's toughest grinder, Ty suffered debilitating lapses in confidence. He couldn't grind his way through a tournament without hiccups that uglied his card with 6s and 7s. His worst shots often came on critical holes down the stretch—the sort of flop the pros call "throwing up on your shoes."

After flying to Malaysia for the Asian Tour's qualifying school in 2005, he had charged out of the gate like Secretariat, shooting 30 for the first nine holes. A birdie putt got him to seven under par through ten holes. With a sand wedge in his hand and another birdie in his sights, he proceeded to scald his wedge shot halfway to Sumatra. A quadruple bogey 9 led to a strange 70, with 30 on the front nine and 40 on the back. Still he earned his way onto the Korean Tour. At one event, "Tryon pulled his tee shot and it landed among rocks," a golf blogger wrote. "He just shrugged. That could have been a sign that he had his emotions under control or, quite simply, that he didn't care."

Bloggers were intrigued by a young woman who followed Ty and often caddied for him. They were inseparable on and off the course. "This is my fiancée, Hanna," Ty said. The two of them had met in Florida. They were a perfect mismatch, the golfer and the Korean-American girl who didn't know a gap wedge from a chairbrella. Their Asian Tour sojourn was a chance for her to reconnect with her roots. But Ty didn't make any money. During the week when his lifeline intersected with Michelle Wie's at the 2006 SK Telecom Open in South Korea, Michelle got $704,303, including $700,000 just for showing up, while Ty got zero. Another missed cut. He had hoped to make a profit playing against weaker fields in Asia, but soon he was $25,000 in the hole. It was time to go home.

Ty and Hanna married in 2006. Later that year she gave birth to a son, Tyson Tryon, a red-faced, black-haired boy who howled his head off, to his young father's delight. "That's my boy," Ty said, grinning. "He's hungry!"

These days Ty cared about every shot. He was playing for his family. "You can't help being changed when you're somebody's husband, somebody's dad," he said. He had sold his Escalade to pay bills, replacing it with a Toyota truck. On the day I caught up with him in May 2007—the same day Sean O'Hair took the first-round lead at the PGA Tour's Byron Nelson Championship—Ty and Hanna and baby Tyson were living in Hobe Sound, Florida, in a condo complex with a pint-size swimming pool. Until recently they'd lived in Orlando and Ty had commuted to Gateway Tour events, driving two and a half hours each way because he couldn't stand to spend a night away from Hanna and Tyson. They moved south to save him the trip, figuring he could scrape up a living on the Gateway Tour.

It wasn't working out. After his flag-kissing tee shot and tap-in birdie, he would finish Tournament #5 in typical Ty fashion: a 71 in the first round, an 81 in the second. Another missed cut. The Gateway Tour slogan is "Where Good Players Become Great," but he was going in the other direction. According to tour official Drew Selden, "He hits it a mile, but something always goes wrong." One Ty-watcher was less kind. "This guy used to be able to get up and down out of a garbage can," a blogger wrote. "These days he's just garbage."

That afternoon, Ty peeked into his condo and whispered to his wife. "Hush," Hanna said. Tyson was asleep. Ty crossed a patch of thirsty Bermuda grass and sat on the steps of a redwood gazebo. He scratched his bearded chin, peering to-

ward a distant row of royal palms. Just past that tree line was
Jupiter Island, the richest zip code in America. Tiger Woods
could moor his $20 million yacht, *Privacy*, at the foot of the
$44.5 million estate he had bought on the far side of those
palms, a little more than a mile from Ty's modest condo. Greg
Norman's beachfront mansion was nearby, too. But Ty's
neighbors were mall-store managers, Jet Ski salesmen, phar-
macists, teachers. Like them, he worried about paying his
bills. His banker father had helped him invest the $2 million
in endorsement money he got after turning pro, and those
investments still spun off enough interest to pay for groceries
and living expenses, but Ty's young family would be hurting
if he couldn't cover his golf-tour expenses. Halfway through
2007, he was $10,000 in the red.

"I'm not that far off," he said, sounding like Michelle
Wie. Sounding, for that matter, like every struggling golfer
since Old Tom Morris got the yips. "One good week—that's
all I need." As he spoke, a three-inch lizard skittered past his
foot. Ty turned his foot to give the lizard room to run. "Last
week, I bogeyed three of the last four holes to miss the cut by
one. I got a little quick coming down from the top, swinging
too hard. But I'm not that far off."

Hearing that his Academy buddy O'Hair was leading the
Byron Nelson, he smiled. "Good for Sean. I hope he wins.
He deserves it."

Ty brightened when I told him what O'Hair had said
about him. "Ty's good enough to be out here on Tour," Sean
had said. "He just needs to keep fighting." O'Hair thought Ty
lacked confidence, not talent—same as Sean five years before.
Confidence and the priceless experience of being in contention at the pro level, being *in the mix* and getting accustomed

to that crucible. Of course that wouldn't be easy for Ty, whose struggles were now as well known as O'Hair's bitter youth. Ty appreciated O'Hair's kind words. At the same time he knew he had become a walking trivia question. *Whatever happened to Ty Tryon?* People who had never met him joked that his middle name wasn't Augustus, it was Keep, as in "Keep Tryon."

He said he was glad he'd turned pro as a teenager: "I thank my parents for helping me make that decision. But it *was* a little crazy. I was a kid out there with Tiger, Ernie, Retief, Sergio. I beat some of 'em a time or two. But it's hard out there on the Tour. You shoot 67 and ten guys shoot 66. The next day maybe you feel stiff or a little nervous and you shoot 75. Now you're ten strokes behind. And you might think, 'Do I really belong here?'

"From as far back as I can remember, I'd set up to hit a putt and picture the ball going in the hole. And then it *did*! When I was sixteen, I shot 60 in a U.S. Open qualifier. I could force a shot—try extra hard and make it happen. This goes on for years and years. It's who you *are*. But then one day it doesn't work. The club feels weird in your hand, so maybe you try harder. And that's wrong, too."

Today, for instance: On a par-five late in the day, he faced a 230-yard approach to a flag three steps from a bunker. The smart play was to aim for the fat part of the green and make birdie—or par at the worst. But Ty tried to make eagle. He smashed a three-metal at that sucker pin, the ball streaking toward the flag, and his gamble almost worked. But the wind wasn't quite right, or maybe his will was too weak to make the ball obey. Or maybe his socks were the wrong color. He'd never been superstitious, but he was starting to think that way. His ball hopped off the back of the green into a row of bushes. Dummyland.

He hadn't had a lesson in more than a year. "I don't want to take another golf lesson as long as I live. I've had enough lessons." He had no swing coach, no mental coach. "I've seen lots of sports psychologists. Obviously, they didn't help." And he had few career options. To Ty, the only thing worse than taking golf lessons would be teaching them. "But I didn't go to college, and I didn't pay too much attention in high school. So I've really got no choice but to work on my golf."

He smiled. Others might see him as a famous flop, but that wasn't how he saw himself. Fatherhood was "awesome, the coolest thing," he said, sounding like O'Hair. In the mornings, before the Florida sun sent man and lizard running for cover, Ty liked to carry baby Tyson around the complex, pointing out birds, bugs, helicopters, sprinklers. He said he wished he could stay home all day. Instead, he went to a range up the road to work on his swing. He was trying to keep himself from rushing it, trying to hold the midswing transition an instant longer, to let the transition mature. If he could save one stroke a round, he could keep the dream alive.

Naptime was almost over. Tyson would be up soon, looking for his dad.

Not every Leadbetter golfer is headed for the PGA Tour or even the minitours. Some come to the Academy with less grandiose ambitions.

Kyle Klempner, a senior at the rigorous St. Stephen's Episcopal School in Bradenton, studied forty hours a week. Klempner, who wore thick spectacles that made him look like a teen accountant, was a decent golfer but no star. He knew he would never tee it up with Tiger, or even with Ty. Instead, he expected his years at the Leadbetter Academy to prepare him for life as a golfing executive, maybe even a CEO. His days were a swirl of golf, classes, homework and more homework. "For me, it's all about time management," he said. "Everything I do—even golf—costs me study time."

Still he sometimes found seven hours to lead a blind man around a golf course. Klempner was a volunteer "sight guide" for golfer Kyle Pinkalla, fifty, a former construction worker who was blinded by a stroke in 1997. A 90-shooter before his stroke, Pinkalla shot 110 in his first United States Blind Golf Association tournament. For nine holes. "But I wasn't about to give up," he says. He and the guide he calls "young Kyle" worked hard over their next dozen rounds—roughly a hundred hours that Klempner could have spent studying. Then Pinkalla's world changed. With young Kyle rattling the flagstick to give him an audible target, Pinkalla holed a putt for a nine-hole 75 that got him into the Blind Golf Association's national finals.

Every golfer should see a USBGA event. "It can be frustrating and it can be long—four hours for nine holes—but it makes you grateful for your vision, and grateful that you can help this blind golfer by setting him up, pointing him in the right direction, and just being his friend," Klempner says.

Pinkalla liked to joke about his disability: "I'm a feel player—obviously," he said. But he was serious about saving strokes. He practiced putting on the carpet in his elderly father's living room, listening for the clink of the ball rolling into a drinking glass. On the course, he listened to his guide. Caddie/guide Klempner would lead Pinkalla to the tee, set him up over over the ball, and then step back to offer some fine-tuning: "Front foot forward a little…back foot left…a little more…back foot forward. OK, you're set."

Blind golfers don't waggle for fear of hitting the ball accidentally, so the Kyles devised another way to beat pre-swing tension. Pinkalla wiggles his toes. "My wiggle waggle," he calls it. During one recent round, he took a smooth, slow backswing and *pow*—hit a screaming hook toward a housing development. Next came a long, excruciating moment. For all he knew, the ball was in the middle of the fairway. Klempner had to deliver the bad news.

"Um…duck hook left," he said. "I hope you didn't hit that house."

"*What* house?"

A few months later, Pinkalla fired a 48 for nine holes—better than the average golfer shoots. "I'm great at the blind approach shot," joked Pinkalla, whose humor often surprised sighted players. He actually convinced a few of them that he could *smell* his way around the course. In fact, like most of us, he visualized every shot. He tried to match his swing to the picture in his mind's eye: "Inside my head, I still see myself throwing the clubhead through the ball, down the line to the target.

"Golf is the most fun thing I do," Pinkalla said. A local charity gave him a scanner that downloaded books into his computer, which then "read" them aloud in a robotic voice. He scanned loads of golf books, from histories to the latest swing tips. "There's a wedge tip I want to try," he said.

Not long ago, Pinkalla was facing a lob-wedge shot from greenside rough, thirty yards from the flag. Klempner helped him set up with his weight forward, clubface open. Pinkalla made a steep swing through total darkness to a spot where he pictured the ball. His wedge slid through the grass, sending the ball on a lazy arc to the green. He heard it land with a soft thud. He listened. And then, a second or two later, he heard a sound every golfer loves. He heard his ball tap the flagstick and clonk into the cup.

SIX

BREAKTHROUGH: THE LAST GIANT STEP

You can be hugely talented and perfectly trained, with rippling muscles driving your lab-tested Leadbetter swing, and still hit the biggest shot of your life down a drainpipe. How can that be? Swing scientist Leadbetter blames the many muscles of the hands for twitching invisibly at the last instant. The maverick swing coach Mac O'Grady once paid for a UCLA study on twitchy hands. People thought he was joking, but the 1989 study, reported in the journal *Neurology*, blamed a neural disorder called focal dystonia that bedevils typists, musicians and painters as well as athletes, making their hand muscles misfire at key moments. The study of more than four hundred amateur and pro golfers found that twitching fingers could be related to obsessive thinking.

Treatments included botox to deaden the nerves. O'Grady rejoiced at being scientifically vindicated, but he kept missing putts. Knowing the demon's name didn't cure his yips.

What happens in the muscles begins in the brain. That's surely why golfers who sail through one level of the game can suffer meltdowns when they reach the next. They don't yet believe they have earned their place. The golfer needs a breakthrough at each new level, an event or series of events that proves he belongs.

But why? The game is pretty much the same at each level. Hit the ball far and straight, roll it to the hole. There's nobody playing defense. PGA Tour courses might be longer and tighter than the ones amateurs play, with pins tucked in dangerous spots, but they're not long and tight and tricky enough to turn teenage Ty Tryon's 66s into bearded Ty's 79s. No, Ty's scores—and Michelle Wie's, and for that matter Tiger's—measure more than skill. Golf scores seem to depend, at least in part, on what golfers feel they deserve.

How can golf mirror a player's mental state? According to David Feherty, who had three top-10 finishes in majors, it has to do with "comfort level." Feherty recalls a moment on a Sunday at the British Open—not down the stretch, but on the front nine. "It occurred to me that if I made another birdie, I could win! And something clicked off. Something made it *not* happen." He believes many golfers shy from hitting the shot that could get them into the mix. "A golfer's mind seeks its comfort level. If you don't make that birdie, you can comfortably finish a great week without going to that scary place where the great players go."

Other insiders told me a golfer's breakthrough is all about character, by which they meant courage, willpower, virtue, chutzpah. Fair enough, but there had to be a cause for the effect—a reason the player's soul leaks out at the moment of truth.

"It's simple," Gary Gilchrist says. "The ball knows what you're thinking."

Mental conditioning wasn't the only way the Bradenton Bunch got a psychic edge on other golfers. Some Academy golfers' parents also paid extra to have a former actor teach their kids how to communicate.

Late in May, after the usual half day of school and half day on the range, several Leadbetter kids headed for a warren of rooms near the swimming pool. Inside, the walls were painted a bright shade of orange called Mango Madness to match the hair color and sunny mood of Steve Shenbaum, whose acting credits included small, wacky roles in *Space Jam* and *American Pie 2*. Shenbaum, thirty-six, ran Game On, a communications clinic that was one of several for-profit businesses on the IMG Academies campus. (Others included the Wellness Spa and Pendleton, the on-campus school.) A sign across his office wall read, COMMUNICATE LIKE A CHAMPION TODAY!

Outsiders often called Game On a media-training program. "Wrong!" Shenbaum said. While the 2 to 3 percent of Academy golfers who turned pro might need help with interviews, "everyone needs to communicate. On job interviews. On dates. In life!" According to Shenbaum, teen golfers are often socially backward. "They're a different animal. I mean, look at American culture. We're fast-paced, we're full of bravado. We're NFL football! But golfers make a strange choice—to be essentially alone for hours at a time. Golf calls for sacrifice, and one thing young golfers sacrifice is social skills."

He and his colleague, Blair Dalton, a bubbly, Rachael Ray-ish brunette, found that they had to work harder with Leadbetter Academy golfers than with IMG athletes who played other sports. "Golfers are observers, not talkers. They watch which way the grass grows," Dalton said. To communicate effectively, "they have to learn to loosen up." She and Shenbaum had helped Peter Uihlein prepare his acceptance speech when he was named the AJGA Player of the Year. They also worked with Paula Creamer, who had been so terrified of giving a thirty-second talk at the trophy ceremony that she used to lose junior tournaments on purpose. Shenbaum and Dalton appealed to peppery Paula's kickassitude. "We said, 'Paula, do you have what it takes to give a kickass speech?'" The answer, after weeks of practice, was a speech so smooth that Creamer calls it a career highlight.

The latest Game On session found Dalton leading half a dozen athletes in an elaborate improv. Five soccer and tennis players bopped around the room, inventing their lines, while the golfer in the group, Christina DeTomasi, held back. "Christina, you're on a cruise ship attacked by pirates," Dalton said. "Make something happen!"

Christina sulked into the action in the middle of the room. At first she behaved like a typical only-child golfer. "If you kill me," she told a pirate, "my mom will be so mad!" The pirate, a muscly tennis player, responded by pinning her arms behind her. Then something happened: In a blur of quick motion she spun sideways and slipped free.

"Where'd she go?"

Out the door. Christina was answering the signal that had triggered her fight-or-flight reflex: answering her cell phone.

On a sun-scorched day at the end of the school year, some of the Leadbetter golfers quit thinking about golf for one night. Eleven stretch limousines cruised onto campus. Boys in tuxes and evening-gowned girls tottering on spike heels came out to meet the limos. It was the night of the Pendleton Prom.

Before the athletes got into the cars, security men checked their pockets, backpacks and purses for contraband. IMG is serious about its role in loco parentis; like the six Pendleton School proms before it, this would be a tobacco-free, alcohol-free party. From Bradenton the limos paraded to Sarasota, around St. Armand's Circle and back to the IMG Academies Golf & Country Club at El Conquistador, better known as El Con. Tanned, fit couples climbed stairs lined with spangled balloons and paper stars. In the ballroom, each table held two long-stemmed white roses in vases a yard high. Black napkins stamped with gold letters carried the night's theme: DON'T FORGET ABOUT US/2007 PENDLETON PROM. After salad, prime rib and soft drinks, a gold-chained DJ got the kids up onto the dance floor.

The girls were as perfectly primped as the Wellness Spa on campus could make them. Many had spent hours in the spa, where manicures cost $35 to $65, facials $80 to $155, a Rosemary Mint Awakening Body Wrap $125 and an Outer Peace Acne Treatment $150. The spa was another of IMG's money centers, but nobody complained during prom week.

Marika Lendl, a prom-queen nominee, was one of the best golfer-dancers. Unlike her younger sister Isabelle, Marika wasn't one to miss a party. Christina DeTomasi, manicured and pink-pedicured, danced up a storm in a short white dress and a stack of golden hair. According to Pendleton valedictorian Taylar Green, dancing skill roughly matches social status on campus, with soccer players at the top, followed by basketballers, baseball players, tennis players and, finally, golfers. Boy golfers in particular tended to dance like storks. A couple of boy golfers slipped into the bar to watch highlights of that day's Players Championship on TV. One of the pros on the TV screen was Sean O'Hair, Pendleton Class of 2000, nondancer.

When English teacher Brett Pottieger announced the crowning of the prom king and queen, both soccer players, there was a flurry of cell-phone photos. Then the lights went multicolored and music shook the windows. It was the grinding hour, when dancers simulate sex, going crotch-to-crotch and crotch-to-butt with a zeal that made Pottieger blush. "They dance suggestively!" he shouted over the music. One boy golfer, flexing his knees, seemed to be finding a new, better use for his center of gravity.

It was all over at 11 p.m. A helium balloon headed for the moon. Promgoers rode the eleven limos one last time—back to the campus parking lot, where couples posed for final cell-phone photos. "C'mon, I gotta hit balls in the morning," someone said. One couple slipped into the shadows for a quick, illicit kiss. Giulia Molinaro stood on the curb, a long-stemmed white rose in her hand. In a quiet moment, she swung the rose in slow motion as if it were a golf club.

As the school year winds down, the junior season heats up. At the end of May, America's best young golfers gathered at the 2007 Thunderbird Invitational, an annual showdown for the junior elite. Philip Francis, who had spent much of the past year trading the number-one ranking with Peter Uihlein, was back to defend his 2006 Thunderbird title. Peter and his buddy Bank Vongvanij flew west from Florida to join eight others from the Bradenton Bunch including Isabelle Lendl, the girls' defending champ. White vans delivered players from the tournament hotel to Grayhawk Golf Club in Scottsdale, Arizona, where jackrabbits and ground squirrels skittered through sandy, sun-baked rough. The vans' doors bore the AJGA's motto, DEVELOPING GOLF'S NEXT GENERATION. As the golfers piled out and made for the practice range, they peered up at a towering white leaderboard that shadowed a pond by the 18th green. Fourteen flags flew over the range, representing the players' home countries. "Big-time," one boy said. "Are we gonna be on TV?"

The temperature was 88 degrees at 8 a.m. Tournament officials handed out *Hydration Tips*, warning players to "*Drink throughout play*," "*Monitor urine color* (Darker yellow indicates the need to increase fluid)" and "*Prepare for Heat Emergency*." The previous evening, the kids had beaten the heat by playing night golf. Pop music blared from fake rocks near the first tee (one player insisted it was "*rock* music—from a rock!") while they punched wedge shots over the pond to the 18th green. The night was full of laughter, flying golf balls, the occasional splash. Nobody won—for once they were playing for fun.

The top junior boys, Francis and Uihlein, were as similar and different as the sides of a shiny new coin. Lanky, laid-back Peter Uihlein, the six-foot-one Titleist scion, had been playing since he was a toddler swinging plastic Fisher-Price clubs at the Titleist balls his father's company made. Fifteen years later, Peter swung hard and chased the ball as if he couldn't wait to subdue the course. His Leadbetter Academy instructor, Tim Sheredy, called him "a throwback, an old-fashioned shotmaker. Peter can hit it high or low, spin it, hit it soft." Steve Shenbaum, the IMG media trainer who worked with Peter on the Bradenton campus, saw the seventeen-year-old as a rich kid with a burden. "He has endless means. His mother flies all over the country with him. His caddie and his swing coach fly with them. But that's its own set of challenges. How would you like to be the rich kid everyone expects to win?"

Peter's swagger rubbed some people wrong. "He's too cocky for my taste," said a veteran of the junior scene, "and his mom is out of control. His mom should be in the clubhouse, having an iced tea."

But Tina Uihlein didn't need tea. Peter's rail-thin mother, who had moved south from Mattapoisett, Massachusetts, to live in a Bradenton condo with her son, carried several bottles of water in her Titleist backpack. Thin and fiftyish, Tina tracked her son like a terrier. Often walking thirty-six holes a day, she was famous for talking at length to his shots: "C'mon, ball, c'mon c'mon...*yes!* Attababy!" She kept track of Peter's putts, greens in regulation and fairways hit as well as his score. When he finished a hole, she flipped out her PDA and shot a text to Wally at work in Massachusetts: *Birdie he's -2!!*

Peter's rival, Philip Francis, eighteen, was smaller, a skinny live wire with energy to burn, and his dad was no corporate chieftan in a business suit. John Francis, fifty-three, favored bucket hats and Harley-Davidson T-shirts. He owned a Slurpee emporium. His 7-Eleven store in Las Vegas featured the usual cold drinks and snacks as well as a bank of blinking, beeping slot machines. Some college coaches called his blonde, sun-bleached son the best prospect since Philip Mickelson. Both Philip Francis and Peter Uihlein had started out like Mickelson and Tiger Woods—watching their fathers hit thousands of balls, then swinging toy clubs as toddlers. Now both of them exuded pleasure in the hunt for junior-golf trophies. Both said the same thing when asked what they loved about the game: "Winning."

Uihlein and Francis were the alpha golfers in any junior event, but both were scuffling as the Thunderbird's final round wore on and the temperature broke 100. Bank Vongvanij, clouting sky-high drives that carried farther in dry desert air, had two strokes on the field as Francis reached the last hole, a par-five. Needing an eagle to have a chance, Philip whammed a 305-yard drive into a fairway bunker. "End of story. He can't reach the green from there," someone said.

"Maybe. Maybe not," said John Francis, whose bucket hat and lobster tan made him look more like a Jimmy Buffett fan than a golf dad. John figured his boy still had a shot at the trophy. "He could make eagle. He's still got a chance, and that's all that boy needs. Ever since he was hitting Wiffle golf balls around our yard, he's been all about doing it better and better."

Philip Francis's first golf experience was sitting in his baby stroller, watching his dad hit balls on the driving range at Spanish Trail Golf Club in Las Vegas. Next came toy clubs and peewee tournaments. Soon, Philip was the world's best ten-year-old golfer. He won the Junior World Championship four years in a row (while John paid a 7-Eleven cashier to cover for him at the store while he drove Philip to San Diego for the tournament). Philip had no worthy rival his age until he ran up against Peter Uihlein, the first junior player he saw as a legitimate rival, if not quite an equal. "Peter took his number-one ranking away for a couple months," John Francis says, "but then Philip took it back, didn't he?"

Taking his stance in a fairway bunker 210 yards from the green, Philip twisted his feet for better footing in the sand. He waggled his six-iron, threatening the ball. The shot made no sense, not with the bunker's lip casting a shadow that almost reached the ball, not with a pond guarding the green. But he could pull it off if the ball barely cleared the lip and held its line. Nine hundred and ninety-nine of a thousand golfers would have felt an iota of doubt, but not Philip, and somehow this conviction passed from his head through his heart and down his six-iron to the telepathic ball, which left blades of grass waving as it zipped a half inch over the bunker's lip.

John Francis had a word for that shot: "Ha!"

Philip watched the ball drop and brake on the green. He grinned and shook his fist at the leaderboard. One of his playing partners praised the shot with the customary word. "Shot," the boy said. The third boy in their group was more effusive: "*Golf* shot."

Peter Uihlein, playing behind him, had just birdied. Philip wouldn't know that until the leaderboard changed. Junior-golf crowds aren't big enough to send roars resounding around the course. Not even Tina Uihlein ("C'mon, Peter, c'mon . . . Yes! *Yes!*") was loud enough to hear from six hundred yards away.

In the end they both fell short by a fingernail. Philip settled for birdie. After Peter's uncooperative Titleist lipped out on the same hole, his buddy Vongvanij had two strokes to play with. Bank, the soul of rectitude, hedged every bet as he struck the last shots of his junior career. At the final tee a tournament official referred to him as "Vonvanovich" as if he were Thai by way of Minsk. Bank looped a mid-iron layup to land short and left of the 18th green, taking the pond out of play. From there he struck a low, safe pitch to the edge of the green and two-putted. As his second putt fell in, he and the ball were both thinking, *Chana leaw ja*, Thai for "I win."

Despite losing that week, Philip Francis and Peter Uihlein were junior golf's leading lights, the stars patriotic fans hoped would help reestablish the United States as the world's leading producer of male golf talent. "The rest of the world has been making us look sick," an American PGA Tour pro told me. While other countries turned out young stars like Australia's Adam Scott and Aaron Baddeley and Colombia's Camilo Villegas, "We've barely got a world-class guy under thirty." Why? Because the United States had no effective national junior program. In Australia and Sweden, promising youngsters got funneled into government-subsidized teaching programs. They got clubs, balls, tee times and top-notch instruction for little or no money. That was why you seldom saw an Aussie or a Swede at the Leadbetter Academy. But in America, it was every family for itself.

Leadbetter loathed the "class warfare" he saw in American golf. "It's fine to say, 'Play golf, America,' but it costs too much," he said. Of course his school wasn't cheap. Despite the scholarships that went to a few phenoms, the Leadbetter Academy was the most profitable part of the IMG Academies, which accounted for about 2 percent of IMG's reported $1 billion in annual revenues.

But what about The First Tee, the well-funded program backed by Shell, Wal-Mart and other sponsors? Leadbetter called it "a wonderful idea" that was "really about character-building, not nurturing talent." Mitchell Spearman, another prominent swing coach, was less politic. "The First Tee is a corporate feel-good program—useless for developing players."

That left promising American golfers to pay their own way as they climbed the ladder through regional tours to the elite, expensive AJGA circuit.

Peter Uihlein got his first victory of the year three weeks after the Thunderbird, at the FootJoy Invitational in Greensboro, North Carolina. After one of the ugliest of the year's uglies in the first round—a 10 on a par-five hole—he set his jaw and spent the next three days climbing back into contention. On the final green, he faced an evil putt of forty feet. He pictured the hole in close-up, big as a manhole, his gleaming beach-ball-size Titleist rolling into tap-in range beside it. Settling into his putting stance, left hand low, he sent the ball swooping right, then left. It finished the way he had pictured it. "Finally!" he said after tapping in. "If that's what it takes, I'll take a ten in every tournament."

Between rounds, he phoned sports psychologist Passarella back in Bradenton. Peter was one of several Leadbetter Academy stars whose families paid extra for private counseling from the mental coach. "Like most males, Peter is very visual," says Passarella. Peter liked to picture his target—a flag or landing area—glowing like a pane of stained glass with the sun behind it. The ball moved toward the glow. As Passarella explains it, a feedback loop between the visual center of a golfer's brain and his swing can affect the swing, making the ball move the way the golfer imagined it moving. "The brain doesn't know the difference between reality and fantasy," says Passarella. In other words, the ball *acts* like it knows what you're thinking.

In July, Peter Uihlein was the favorite in the U.S. Junior Amateur. The tournament was the jewel of the junior schedule. Regional qualifying had winnowed more than 3,000 entrants down to 156. Tournament volunteers met golfers and their families at Lambert–St. Louis International Airport and helped them find their way through cornfields to Boone Valley Golf Club. Yellow banners greeted the players, just as at the U.S. Open and other USGA championships. A white column at the gate listed previous winners, including Johnny Miller (1964), David Duval (1989) and Tiger Woods (1991–1993). The course, a P.B. Dye layout that hosted a Champions Tour event from 1996 to 2001, had been lengthened by three hundred yards to challenge today's juniors. The insides of the cups had been spray-painted white to show up on TV.

Brandel Chamblee, a PGA Tour veteran, was covering the event for the Golf Channel. Chamblee, forty-five, was an old-school Texan who wasn't impressed by the swings he saw at Boone Valley. "Long swings with long clubs," he said. "These kids are so mechanical." He knew the world had changed the first time he saw Tiger Woods freeze during a practice swing so that he could examine his own elbow position, something Ben Hogan or Jack Nicklaus would never have done. He admired Leadbetter but worried that the

Leadbetter Academy and its imitators were turning out "golf robots" with million-dollar swings and ten-cent hearts. When the young robots reached pro golf, with its glass-fast greens, tucked pins, and relentless, do-or-die pressure, they tended to go haywire.

"There's still an essence to the game that's hard to teach," Chamblee said. "Maybe you have to learn it yourself."

The hottest stick coming into the Junior Amateur was clotheshorse Mu Hu, who reached Boone Valley by dominating a qualifying tourney in Tennessee. Mu made twenty birdies in thirty-four holes in the qualifier, the junior performance of the year. It was a measure of his promise as well as his volatility that he capped that dazzling thirty-four-hole stretch with an ugly. He finished the qualifier bogey, triple bogey—and still won by nine. Once again he was playing like the kid who'd been lionized as China's Tiger since he won his country's Junior Golf Open as an eleven-year-old. Mu welcomed the comparison, and with the cockiness of youth reckoned he could outstyle the game's fashion leader if not outplay him. "Tiger's a great, great player," he told me, "but not that great a dresser. He could match his colors better."

At the 2006 HSBC Champions tournament in Shanghai, a reporter had asked Woods about China's golfers. "Of course I have heard of Mu Hu," Woods said. "Chinese golf is growing fast—with the advent of videoing golf swings and getting proper instruction at an early age, you're seeing kids progress faster than they ever have in sports history." To promote the tournament, he teamed with Mu in a Ping-Pong match against European Tour pros Paul Casey and David Howell. "We crushed 'em," says Mu. "I played defense and Tiger smashed balls they couldn't touch."

After post-Ping-Pong handshakes and fist bumps, he got a private moment with Woods. Mu's mother had told him to ask for advice: How can a talented boy reach his potential? But Mu had his own agenda.

"Tiger," he said. "How many cars do you have?"

Mu was spiffy as ever at the 2007 Junior Amateur. Almost all the other kids wore shorts, but Mu, as always, played in long pants. His crimson slacks matched his shoes, shirt, hat and even his tees. But his ball wasn't so much telepathic as bipolar. 4th in a field of 156 after two rounds of medal play, he promptly flamed out in the initial round of match play, taking a six-and-four drubbing. Mu was the unfinished phenom: He had doting parents, a gorgeous swing and an iffy short game. He also had a troubling penchant for the sudden collapse.

Peter Uihlein was a step ahead of Mu. Peter had proved himself in junior competition. Peter seldom suffered from the sudden collapse. Even his 10 at the FootJoy Invitational was a hiccup. He had come back to win the tournament, after all. At the Junior Amateur, the kid the Golf Channel's Chamblee called "the best junior player in America" covered his sandy-blonde curls with a Titleist cap that had the Leadbetter logo on the side. Even at seventeen, Peter knew how to prioritize his loyalties.

He had flown in from Florida with his mother and a cigarette-smoking professional caddie. Tanned Tina Uihlein, looking thin and brittle as a cinnamon stick, hurried after her boy as he won his first two matches. She handed him a banana and marched two hundred yards ahead. She called "Stop, stop, sit sit sit" when one of his drives bounced toward the rough, and gave him the "safe" sign like an umpire when it stayed in the fairway.

Late in his match against Jeffrey Kang, the golf-prodigy son of a Korean studio musician, Peter reached the toughest hole on the course, a 477-yard par-four. He bopped a 340-yard drive that rolled downhill to the lip of a pond. From there he faced an uphill approach over the water. Taking a practice swing, Peter imagined the flagstick glowing like a Disney World lightstick. He took dead aim. He sent a wedge shot skyward, divot flying, the ball tracing a tall arc to a landing two feet beyond the hole. His mother gasped, "Oh. My. God." as Peter's Pro V1 bit the green and sucked back like a ball on a string, straight into the hole. Eagle.

Peter hoisted his wedge with both hands as if it were Excalibur. He had clinched the match. He knew it, Kang knew it, the Golf Channel audience knew it, moments later Wally Uihlein, reading an ecstatic text from Tina, knew it, and so, perhaps, did the ball, nuzzling the flagstick at the bottom of the hole.

But Peter wouldn't win the Junior Amateur. The finalists would be a couple of younger boys who putted better than he did in the next round.

Academy students spend long hours on putting drills. Some sharpen their strokes by shrinking the target, aiming at tees planted in the green instead of at cups. Others employ a drill that tests Tour pros—make sixty three-footers in a row before you leave the green. Still, putting is what Leadbetter calls "a bit of a mystery." Less susceptible to analysis than the full swing but no less important, the putting stroke bedeviled full-swing geniuses from Old Tom Morris to Ben Hogan to Sam Snead long before yips-addled Mac O'Grady ever heard of focal dystonia. Hogan, who called putting "the game within the game," once yipped a one-foot putt thirty feet past the hole. Snead tried a sidesaddle putting style that was ruled illegal. Chris DiMarco beat his yips by switching to a "claw" grip that made him look like he was strangling his putter. Ky Laffoon, a tour pro in the thirties who nicknamed his putter "son of a bitch," punished it by tying it to the bumper of his car, driving off and laughing as the S.O.B. bounced along behind him, kicking up sparks.

At the 2007 Junior Amateur, a shy Texan named Anthony Paolucci rolled in a ten-foot putt to knock off Peter Uihlein in the week's biggest upset. But soon Paolucci, fourteen, was losing in the semifinals to a tough, unsmiling eighteen-year-old, Sean Brannan, who was known as a deadeye putter. As Brannan stroked a six-footer for the win, Paolucci stepped up to offer him a handshake before the putt reached the hole. But the ball stayed out. Thus began the putting misadventure of the year.

On the last hole, Brannan had yet another putt to win. This one measured thirty inches. He tapped it...out! They went to extra holes. The first was a par-five. Paolucci dubbed his second shot, which hopped forward forty-five yards. Two more swings left him twenty-five feet above the hole, lying four, while Brannan lay three a yard from the cup. Paolucci kept it interesting—his long putt trickled into the cup. Now Brannan settled over his three-footer. Did the ball know what he was thinking? Did it think, *I might miss*?

Again Paolucci removed his hat, preparing to offer the victor a handshake. Again, somehow, Brannan shoved the ball past the hole. At the next and last hole, he lagged a dicey approach putt to eighteen inches. A kick-in. The ball horseshoed around the cup and stayed out. Sean Brannan lost. He went home to Hollidaysburg, Pennsylvania, with the memory of four easy putts horseshoeing around in his head.

In the final, Paolucci's own putter turned to putty as he fell to fifteen-year-old Corey Whitsett, the surprise Junior Amateur champion, who had the putting week of his young life.

If golf is the most mental sport, putting is the most mental part of the most mental sport. The least understood, the least coachable, the loneliest.

"Michelle's been working hard," Leadbetter said. "She putts and putts and putts." On the practice green, Michelle Wie made everything. On the course, she missed everything important. It was almost enough to make you believe in the telepathic golf ball.

Michelle needed a breakthrough at the 2007 LPGA Championship. Instead, the fading phenom finished last among those who made the cut—thirty-five strokes behind winner Suzann Pettersen, ten shots out of next-to-last place. Her wrist ached, but she played on despite Leadbetter's urging that she rest and regroup. Lead and manager Greg Nared were often cut out of the Wies' decision-making process. "It's out of my hands," said Nared. "The player makes the decision when she plays."

Michelle managed to look unprofessional even compared to amateurs. At Sorenstam's tournament MacKinzie Kline, a fifteen-year-old amateur with a heart defect that drained her energy, struggled to an 89 that left her on the wrong side of Rule 88. Had she considered withdrawing instead of finishing, as Michelle had done? "No, you have to keep playing no matter what you shoot," she said. Young MacKinzie, who breathed oxygen through a tube during her round, made mighty Michelle look like the one who lacked heart.

Team Wie hoped Michelle would turn her year around at the U.S. Women's Open. Her first round scotched that idea. Walking with a physical therapist who massaged her wrist between shots, she shot 82. Yet even after hitting a drive out of bounds, losing one in the bushes, pulling an approach shot sixty yards left of the green and scattering her gallery with several others, she made excuses. "It's a very fine line between shooting 69 and shooting what I shot today," she announced. By then she had not broken 70 in a tournament round in nearly a year. "I'm not that far off," she said.

The following day, after an ugly front-nine 42 left her 17 over par through twenty-seven holes, Michelle clanked the first drive of her back nine into a row of pines. Her shoulders sagged. With no shot at the green, she punched her ball back to the fairway. Then, once again, she gave up. Soon the Wies were pulling out of the parking lot with B.J. at the wheel. As in the nursery rhyme, they went Wie, Wie, Wie all the way home. *Golf World*'s Ron Sirak expressed the pundits' consensus, calling for an end to the "Michelle Wie soap opera.... How can this sort of public humiliation be good for the confidence of a teenager trying to grow up on a public stage?"

Enter Gary Gilchrist, Michelle's swing coach until he split with Leadbetter in 2003. Gilchrist, emboldened by his student Pettersen's win at the LPGA Championship, blamed Leadbetter for Michelle's troubles and offered to replace his old boss as her coach. In private, he and Lead weren't so far apart. Both men had both known Michelle since she was twelve. Both saw her as a unique talent, no less remarkable than Tiger Woods had been. What was remarkable was how completely such a talent could be screwed up. But the reason was clear to all who'd followed her roller-coaster journey: For all her talent, she had risen too far too soon.

Gilchrist cast himself as a lone voice of reason. Players like Michelle "hear one thing from their parents, another from their agent, another from their coach. They need someone to tell them the *truth*," he told me. "Michelle should have stayed in the hot kitchen," the toughening process Paula Creamer and other phenoms endured, competing with kids their own age. Gilchrist had never forgotten a moment at the Academy when B.J. Wie pulled him aside, nodded toward Paula and said, "Look how much stronger mentally she is than Michelle!"

Now Gilchrist made news by blasting Leadbetter, telling reporters Michelle's swing had never looked worse. She was "hitting it everywhere." He publicly offered his services to Michelle and her parents. If the Wies dumped Leadbetter, he said, "we could come up with some agreement."

Reporters ran to Lead, who said, "Gary learned all his stuff from me. I'll leave it at that." Privately, though, he was shaking his head. "I helped bring Gary into this profession. Now he kicks me in the teeth."

Gilchrist may be a tireless self-promoter, but he truly believed his former boss was filling Michelle's head with swing diagrams when she needed to relax. There was a term for what Leadbetter's critics called his overly mechanical approach. The term was "Lead poisoning," and Gilchrist thought Michelle Wie was Lead's latest victim. But he knew his former boss wasn't really the villain in this soap opera.

Michelle had no business playing golf. Her mad-dash

schedule had worn her out. Her injured wrists were affecting her swing. She was flinching at impact, trying to generate power with a last-second lunge that sent hooks and blocks flying in every direction while her few straight drives carried 230 yards instead of 280. Still her parents pushed her to press on, and Michelle was on their side. She wanted to play, insisted on playing, to prove her worth to her corporate sponsors and to prove she belonged at the game's highest level.

Michelle Wie thought she needed a professional breakthrough, but maybe she needed a personal breakthrough as well. Maybe she needed the courage or willpower or drive that Sean O'Hair summoned up on the day he finally said no to his domineering dad.

Nick Price has vivid memories of his breakthrough. Price, the former World Junior champion who would go on to win three majors, was already twenty-five when he asked Lead to remake his swing. Four months later he led the 1982 British Open at Royal Troon. Three shots ahead with only six holes to play, he fumbled the lead away.

Crushed? He was elated. "The biggest moment of my golfing life," he calls it, "bigger than my first major. I felt so encouraged because I knew I *could* win. It was only my lack of experience that stopped me."

Leadbetter thought so, too. That night he said, "Nick, now you know you're going to succeed."

Not soon, though. Price's next big chance didn't come until six years later, in the 1988 British Open at Royal Lytham & St. Annes. He felt ready. "I knew that if I got in the hunt on

Sunday, I'd be no stranger to it." He battled Seve Ballesteros down the Sunday stretch, ripping a three-iron to the green at the par-five seventh and holing the putt for eagle. But Ballesteros eagled the same hole. Meanwhile Faldo, the defending champion, was missing putts and grumbling. It seemed Faldo had given up. Price knocked his approach to two inches at the 13th. Birdie. Ballesteros fired a nine-iron to kick-in distance at the 16th. Birdie and a one-shot lead. On the final hole, with Seve in trouble, Price hit a six-iron from the middle of the fairway. He zeroed in on the flag, seeing nothing but the flag, but was so eager to hit the shot that he rushed it. "I always tended to get a little quick when I was excited," he says. In his zeal to hit the shot of his life, he brought the worn face of his six-iron to impact a split second too soon. "Pulled it!" His ball found the green, but it was thirty feet left of the hole. The spell broken, he three-putted to lose by two.

Once again Price felt he had climbed a rung. He had proved he could go toe-to-toe with the great Ballesteros with the world watching. He had failed but hadn't folded. And he made no excuses. That was crucial. Price would come to believe that owning up to failure was the only way to learn from it. He believed golf was like life in that way: It was largely a fight to control fear. Not to deny our fears but to admit them to ourselves, to incorporate them, and try like hell anyway.

Still, Price asked himself, "Am I ever going to win a major?" He was getting tired of moral victories. Leadbetter pounded home the message that moral victories matter more in golf than in other sports because they tend to presage breakthroughs, but Price was starting to wonder. He was starved for what he calls "a *victory* victory."

Persistence, persistence, persistence.

Four years later, Price was thirty-five years old and 0-for-35 in the majors. He was in his sixteenth year as a pro on the day he worked his way to the lead at the 1992 PGA Championship at Bellerive Country Club in St. Louis. The other leaders were spitting the bit, giving Price his best chance yet. Gene Sauers and Jeff Maggert, both playing balls that seemed to know they weren't ready to be major-winners, went backward down the stretch. Maggert played his last seven holes in five over par. That left Price, who had started the round two shots off the lead, standing over his tee shot at the par-three 16th with a chance to win a major at last. Deuces were wild: He had a two-iron in his hands; the hole measured 222 yards; a deuce on the hole would almost surely win him the major he had sought for so long.

Win or lose. Here and now. This was the moment Peter Uihlein, Isabelle Lendl, Mu Hu and every other prodigy would have to master if they proved good enough to reach it: Step up and hit the shot that means breakthrough or defeat.

Don't hurry it, Price thought. The lesson he had learned at Royal Lytham.

He pured his two-iron, sending his brave, confident ball on a low arc to birdie range. He holed the putt and coasted to a three-shot triumph over Sauers, Faldo and two others and then, as often happens, his breakthrough led to a stretch in which he played better than ever before. In 1993 Price won four tournaments and was the PGA Tour's player of the year. In 1994, trailing Jesper Parnevik at the British Open, he sized up a fifty-foot eagle putt at the penultimate hole. "We haven't made a long putt all week," he said, smiling at his caddie.

"Let's give it a shot." The ball trundled downhill, breaking nearly a foot to the right as if sniffing for the hole, and crept in. After Parnevik bogeyed the 18th, Price claimed the Claret Jug at last. He made it back-to-back majors a month later at the 1994 PGA. Nicholas Raymond Liege Price was now the number-one golfer on earth.

Price, who was inducted into the World Golf Hall of Fame in 2003, has thought long and hard about the slow-motion breakthrough that got him there. "Experience is the main thing—being in the mix enough times," he says. "Even if you lose, you've been there. You've felt that pressure before. It's like a chemical process that changes you." He saw the toughening of golfers as a function of pressure, like the hardening of coal into diamond. "It's not just that you're mentally tougher. It's technical, too, since all your work on the practice range enters your thinking in the tee box. Because when you get right down to it, what is confidence? Not just some sunny feeling. It's certainly not the belief you can hit every shot perfectly. Tiger never did that on his best day. For me, the key was getting my swing so sound that I could hit fifty out of fifty drives in play. It might be forty in the fairway, five in the left rough, and five in the right rough, but there'd be *none* out of bounds. At that point I told myself it was a matter of time—if I could get myself back in the mix, sooner or later I was going to win."

Price was perhaps the best ballstriker to come along between Sam Snead and Tiger Woods, but he spent fifteen years in and out of the mix before he won a major. That wasn't all due to his faltering at Troon and Royal Lytham. There was another factor at work: The golfers on the leaderboard in those fifteen years included tough customers named Nicklaus, Watson, Ballesteros, Faldo and Woods.

The last breakthrough is the hardest not only because the courses are tougher and the pressure more intense at the game's highest level, but because the other players are tougher and more intense, too. They have all gone through the chemical change Price endured. Whoever you are, they are tougher than you.

Until the day you prove you belong.

Sean O'Hair took a one-stroke lead into the final round of the richest Tour event of all, the Players Championship. It was a Sunday in May 2007—Mothers' Day. Sean's mother, Brenda, was driving across Florida to Ponte Vedra Beach to follow her son and Phil Mickelson in the final group. Brenda O'Hair was a quiet person, like Sean. Bashful, people said— the opposite of her husband, Marc, who stayed away from Sean's tournaments.

The Players wasn't one of the pro game's four majors, but it was the next-best thing: a so-called "fifth major" with crowds of fifty thousand a day, millions of TV viewers and a Tour-topping first prize of $1.62 million. Twenty-four-year-old Sean had his swing grooved that day, the club in sweet sync with his body's rotation, but he kept missing birdie putts. As he and Mickelson reached the 17th hole at the Tournament Players Club at Sawgrass, O'Hair was two shots behind.

The 17th at Sawgrass is one of the most famous—or notorious—holes in golf. It's the closest the real game has to the crazy-hard fantasy hole on the poster in Charlie Winegardner's bedroom. A short par-three with an island green, it creates splashy drama every year. Golf fans love the hole because the difference between birdie and quadruple bogey often comes down to blind, thrilling luck. Tour pros hate the 17th at Sawgrass for the same reason. "A gimmick," Tiger Woods called it—one of the pros' printable descriptions of architect Pete Dye's do-or-die hole.

Sean O'Hair had a clear choice that sunny afternoon. He could hit a wedge to the fat part of the green—the safe play. Or he could shoot for the flag with a nine-iron, risking watery doom in hopes of making birdie. Mickelson, hitting first, laced a wedge to safety—the luxury of a man with a two-shot lead. O'Hair could do the same and stake his claim to the Tour's richest runner-up paycheck: $972,000, almost double what he had earned all year so far.

"I'm not playing for second," he said.

Caddie Steve Lucas—his cigar-chewing father-in-law—handed Sean his nine-iron, and here came Sean O'Hair's make-or-break moment. Standing on the tee at the 17th at Sawgrass with the wind whipping sideways, squinting through slanting sunlight at the green, he heard his father-in-law say it was 136 yards to the flag. Sean teed up his ball. He took four steps back to peer at the target, a yellow flag perched on a ledge on a little green island. His pre-shot routine hadn't changed: He twirled his nine-iron and took four steps back to the ball.

His swing was perfect. No hurry, no flinch. In that moment, with Mickelson standing three yards away and the whole golf world watching, Sean O'Hair came through. This was pure contact, the ball tracing a high arc toward the flagstick. Sean O'Hair had beaten his demons and made one of the best swings of 2007. Gary Gilchrist might have called that pure contact the result of pure thought: The ball knew what Sean was thinking.

But the wind didn't. Sean's ball hung in the air half a second too long. The wind shifted, adding a foot or two of carry to the shot of his life, which bounced off the back of the green. Splash!

O'Hair swooned, head down, hands on his knees. He was the picture of defeat on a million TVs. He trudged to the drop zone seventy yards from the green, punched a wedge shot that ran off the green, through the fringe and into the drink again. He dropped another ball in the drop zone, lying four. He swung again and this ball held the green. He two-putted for a quadruple bogey 7, then bogeyed the 18th to finish six strokes behind Mickelson, the winner. Sean O'Hair's misadventure at 17 cost him $747,000.

So why was he smiling an hour later?

"People can say I choked or I was scared," he said in the press room. "But I wasn't. I wasn't scared of Phil. I wasn't scared of winning. To win, I had to go for the pin."

A reporter asked Mickelson if he felt empathy for Sean O'Hair. But Mickelson, a three-time major-winner who had learned when to go for broke on Sunday afternoons, shook his head. "It's not empathy. It's respect," he said.

In the clamor of the finish, one moment went unnoticed. After O'Hair watched his tee ball at the 17th, loving the shot, expecting it to scare the flag, only to see it carry too far and hop into the water, he bent at the waist, crushed. This was golf at its cruelest—perfect contact that backfired, a dart through his heart. Fifteen minutes later O'Hair and his father-in-law were walking up the 18th fairway while the crowd cheered Mickelson, the winner. Sean was shaking his head, thinking about the disaster at 17. Then Lucas, lugging his son-in-law's golf bag, told Sean something Marc O'Hair should have said.

He said, "Sean, I'm proud of you."

EPILOGUES

❖

TO BE CONTINUED . . .

Annie Park, the "tween-age" star of the Mike Bender Golf Academy for Korean kids, slumped in the fall of 2007. "It gets boring playing girls my own age," she said.

At one tournament, several Anglo parents accused Annie's mother, who speaks almost no English, of giving her daughter advice in Korean. "She was ten shots ahead at the time!" Annie's older sister, Bora, said. "We understood—they were trying to stand up for their kids—but I hate when it gets racial."

Annie admired the LPGA's Seoul sisters, but disliked being pigeonholed as an "ethnic" golfer. She spoke better Korean than big sister Bora—but never around English-speakers—and made a point of saying her heroes were "Lorena and Annika," not Se Ri Pak.

In the fall, her mother returned to New York, leaving twelve-year-old Annie alone in their Florida condo. "We want her to learn independence," said Bora. The Bender Academy provided a female caretaker to cook for Annie and drive her to school, but beyond that she was on her own. Before and after school, she worked out in the gym and hit balls on the range, dreaming of winning the 2015 LPGA Rookie of the Year award.

Blind golfer **Kyle Pinkalla** spent the winter at his father's house in Wisconsin. "It's too cold to play, and you can only clean your clubs so many times," he said. Like a lot of Midwesterners, he was waiting for April and the start of a new golf season. He loved to "watch" the Masters, listening for the voices of Jim Nantz and David Feherty. "Meanwhile I'm moving to Madison to be with my girlfriend, Linda." They haven't set a wedding date, "but it's getting serious."

IMG vice president **Ted Meekma** announced that the David Leadbetter Golf Academy and Nick Bollettieri Tennis Academy would open branches in Dubai. The schools would be based at Dubai Lifestyle City, the residential heart of Dubailand, a $20 billion "theme world" complete with autodrome, polo club, 600-foot Ferris wheel, the world's largest shopping mall and the first golf course designed by Tiger Woods.

Despite his vow to remain an amateur until 2009, sixteen-year-old **Tadd Fujikawa** turned pro in July 2007. "My parents aren't sure it's the right decision, but I've told them I really want to do this," he announced. "They just have to trust me."

His junior-golf rivals rolled their eyes. "Tadd did it because his endorsement value is high right now," said one. "Why come back to junior golf and get beat?"

As a pro, Fujikawa accepted sponsors' exemptions to nine pro events. He missed the cut in all nine. At least he went out with a bang at the European Masters in September. On his last hole, a 628-yard par-five, the five-foot-one, 130-pounder socked a 343-yard drive, followed by a 285-yard three-wood that hopped into the hole for a double-eagle deuce. It was only the third albatross all year on the European Tour.

Scottish lass **Carly Booth** wasn't happy at the Leadbetter Academy. Her instructor there, Malcolm Joseph, was intent on tweaking her swing. She tested his patience by grumbling and skipping weight-room workouts. Fourteen-year-old Carly also enjoyed playing the game more than beating balls on the range, and didn't like waiting around for an IMG shuttle bus to take her through security to El Con. At a tournament one weekend, ten over par, lonely and miserable, she walked off the course and phoned her brother, Wallace: "I want to go home!"

Back in Comrie, Scotland, she bounced back almost immediately. In July, Carly won the Girls' European Young

Masters. She won a junior event in Dubai. Swinging hard, her blonde locks flowing behind her, she claimed the Scottish Girls' Championship for players under eighteen. At the Ladies' Scottish Open, playing against European professionals, she was low amateur, tying for thirteenth place.

She told me it had been a relief to escape the Leadbetter Academy, where "everyone has to swing the same." Now her handicap was a gaudy plus-3. But the first chill of autumn reminded her of the old line about Scottish weather: "There are two seasons in Scotland, winter and July 21." Help came from golf-resort mogul Lyle Anderson, who had heard about the phenom Scottish newspapers called "our great girl golfer." He and the Booths arranged to send her to Superstition Mountain, an Anderson-owned resort in Arizona.

Mike Malaska, who runs a golf school at Superstition Mountain, thought so much of Carly that he practically adopted her. In October she moved in with Malaska, his wife and their seventeen-year-old daughter, Ashley, with Anderson paying her expenses. Malaska called the arrangement "one of a kind. Imagine sending your kid to *live with* David Leadbetter, Rick Smith or Jim Flick! But it's good for us all." Now fifteen, Carly became fast friends with Ashley and got daily, individual attention from her new coach as well as easy access to two Superstition Mountain courses. She was so happy—and so committed to a new fitness-and-flexibility program—that she did handstands. "She walks around the house on her hands, giggling," said Malaska.

He wasn't planning on taking in any more golfers—or getting rich anytime soon on this one. "It's an investment in the future," Malaska told me, "because Carly can be a superstar. She's as good as Michelle Wie was at fifteen, if not better.

She could be the Tiger Woods of women's golf." He had measured her clubhead speed at a tour-level 110 miles per hour; she was driving the ball 265 yards on the fly. In March 2008, Carly was named to the Great Britain & Ireland Curtis Cup team—the youngest player ever to receive that honor.

Life in America could be "a bit lonely," Carly admitted. She reckoned she could stand it because "the golf's better and so will the money be, when I turn pro." Meanwhile she was loving the weather in Arizona, the malls, and the strange way Americans talk. She liked to call home and startle her parents by saying, "Mum and Dad, *wassup?*"

Nick Price and **Nick Faldo** became senior golfers in 2007. Price turned fifty in January 2007, while Faldo hit fifty in July. Both men were casualties of golf technology—balata-ball hitters who couldn't drive the ball far enough to keep up with the 300-yard generation. Price, the best ballstriker of his generation, lost his advantage when the Titleist Pro V1 and other new balls deemphasized touch in favor of sheer ball-smashing power. In a winless rookie year on the senior-citizens' Champions Tour, he finished fortieth on the money list.

In 2001, Faldo dumped college golfer Brenna Cepelak—who retaliated by smashing his $200,000 Porsche with a nine-iron, doing $20,000 worth of damage—and made travel agent Valerie Bercher his third wife. On the course, his smooth swing was no match for the power he saw in younger players. The modern swing looked to him "like a martial-arts move." So he shifted gears. In 2006, Faldo landed the top job in TV golf, replacing Lanny Wadkins in the CBS booth. Suddenly "Nasty Nick" was the voice of golf. In his new role he morphed into an affable, quotable fellow—you'd love to buy him a pint.

I asked Faldo about his dark days as "Foldo," when he turned himself over to Leadbetter, who remade his swing and made him hit thousands of range balls. "If I had it to do over, I wouldn't," Faldo said. "I'm very lucky I didn't get hurt." But that's the voice of a wealthy TV announcer with six majors on his résumé. More likely, if Faldo flashed back to his years in Lead's intensive care unit, years that transformed him from talented flop to golf immortal, he might listen even harder to the man who helped make him a champion.

Fair-haired **Philip Francis**, one of the top teen stars since Mickelson, graduated from the AJGA to UCLA. At first the hyper, disorganized freshman had a tough transition to college life. He couldn't manage his laundry, let alone his time. He arrived expecting to practice at storied Bel-Air Country Club, where the Bruins play home matches, but he was turned away. The team plays at Bel-Air but isn't allowed to practice there. With two hours between classes that day, he found himself driving an hour and twenty minutes to practice at another course, the Wilshire Country Club. When he arrived, it was past time to turn around and head back to Westwood.

His game didn't suffer. In October, at the Reynolds Plantation resort in Georgia, Philip won the first match of his college career. His father, John, was thrilled—not so much about the win as the way his boy got there. "They fly the team to the tournament and the school pays." John Francis, the Las Vegas 7-Eleven owner, wasn't one of junior golf's wealthy dads. When he traveled to see his son play, he was still paying an employee to cover his shift at the store. "But *he's* got a free ride to UCLA," John crowed. "What's that worth, a couple hundred grand? He'll play fifteen or sixteen tournaments a year, great competition on great courses, and it's free!"

In his second match as a UCLA Bruin, Philip was all but beaten, two holes down with two to play. An older teammate called him aside and said, "No problem. Just be clutch." Philip nodded. *Just be clutch*. His specialty.

He needed a birdie to stay alive. He faced a 230-yard shot over water through a 25-mile-an-hour wind. He pulled a two-iron, waggled, swung hard, watched the ball cut through the wind on its way to the green. Made his birdie. Knocked in a 12-foot putt on the last hole to tie the match. Twenty minutes later he won the match in sudden death. Philip Francis was 2–0 as a college golfer.

Titleist scion **Peter Uihlein**, Francis's top rival in junior golf, dreamed of being a Cowboy. Early in 2007, the tall golden boy announced that he would play his college golf at Oklahoma State. First he told Bank Vongvanij, then he called Cowboys coach Mike McGraw with the good news. But the decision wasn't official until he signed a letter of intent in November. In the meantime Peter won his second AJGA Player of the Year award, and left little doubt his college choice would stick. All summer he wore orange and black, the OSU colors, and swung a driver with an orange and black shaft. His driver cover was a furry Pistol Pete, the mustachioed OSU mascot.

With Pistol Peter joining his junior-golf pals Rickie Fowler and Kevin Tway (son of pro Bob Tway, the 1986 PGA

Tour Player of the Year) in coach McGraw's 2008 lineup, the Cowboys had the look of a dynasty. The kids would try to keep up with seniors Jonathan Moore and Trent Leon, a pair of Leadbetter Academy alums who had led the team to the 2006 NCAA title.

Was Peter Uihlein the next college golf hero or only the second-best prospect of the year, after Philip Francis? There was no consensus. Gary Van Sickle of *Sports Illustrated* pegged Peter as "a good little player" with a long way to go, while Gary Gilchrist called him a future superstar: "Before he's done, Peter Uihlein will be one of the top players in the world."

No other teen golfer combined so much talent, grit, teaching and platinum-plated support. And unlike Tadd Fujikawa, who was not on his level as a prospect, Peter wasn't in a hurry to turn pro. Best of all, he wanted to *earn* his way to the top. He couldn't escape the implications of his surname—people thought he had it easy—but he had been one of the hardest workers at the Academy.

"I like the fight in him," said OSU coach McGraw. "Peter did *not* dominate junior golf. He's got a lot to prove yet. But you know what? I have a soft spot for kids who want to sweat and fight to get better. That's what I see in Peter. He's driven. I may need to say 'Whoa' to calm him down, but I won't have to say 'Giddyup.'"

One lazy afternoon on the Leadbetter range, Peter was smacking mid-irons with his lanky, elbow-y swing. "Oh yeah!" he said when one carried a couple yards farther than the last. His pleasure was the joy of a boy with a limitless future. "I want to win four NCAA championships, then go pro," he said. "Won't that be a blast?"

Despite his flop at the Players Championship, **Sean O'Hair** had a solid 2007 season on the PGA Tour. He played twenty-eight Tour events and finished in the top twenty-five half the time, a ratio matched only by Woods, Mickelson and a few other big names. Yet his results were puzzling in light of his statistics: Despite ranking first on Tour with fifteen eagles, eighth in total driving and sixth in the Tour's all-around stat, O'Hair was only thirty-eighth on the money list, earning a little under $2 million. And he didn't win all year.

"Losing isn't fun," he said, "but trying to win is."

In March 2008, O'Hair shot a gritty final-round 69 to win the PGA Tour's PODS Championship. His second Tour victory earned him $954,000. By then, the shy former misfit was writing a blog for pgatour.com.

Charlie Winegardner finished seventh in a field of eighty-four at an AJGA event in New Mexico. He would have finished higher if not for an incident in the first round: On the first hole, he knocked his drive through the fairway into rocky rough. He was standing over his recovery shot, starting his backswing, when the ball moved. No one else saw it, but Charlie did the right thing. He called a penalty on himself. When Tom Winegardner heard about the penalty, he was quietly proud of his son.

A month later, Charlie left the Leadbetter Academy. For the Winegardners, the Academy had been too expensive and impersonal. "I wasn't so happy with my instructor, but it was good overall," Charlie said. "Playing every day, seeing how the

best junior players in the world get it done, you can't help getting better." In the fall he was back at the Calverton School in
Huntingtown, Maryland, playing guard for the basketball
team. He would take the winter off competitive golf—practice
with his dad, let his mom pamper him—then "hit the tournaments hard in the spring and get ready for college golf." In the
fall of 2008, Charlie would be a freshman at Coastal Carolina
University in Conway, South Carolina.

He had no plans to change his baseball grip.

Fatherhood agreed with **Ty Tryon**, who seemed happiest
when talking about his little boy, Tyson. But his struggles on
the course continued. Ty missed sixteen straight cuts on the
Gateway Tour before finally making a cut in August. Even
then he staggered at the end. Three under par as he played
the last hole, seemingly safe, he triple-bogeyed to make the
cut by a single stroke. He won $1,008 that week.

Tyson Tryon celebrated his first birthday in the fall—
within days of his dad's last tournament of the season. That
event, Tournament 12 of the Gateway Tour's Beach Summer
Series, was a small moral victory for Ty, who fired a second-
round 67 to make the cut. But on the last day, after a deuce at
the 223-yard 16th hole, he double-bogeyed the 18th for a
season-ending 79. He finished forty-sixth and won $941.

For the year, he made five cuts in twenty-five tries and
earned a total of $5,610. He was still only twenty-three, but
his money was running out.

I asked Ty what he would do if Tyson turned out to be a
golf phenom. He said he'd want his boy to have a chance to

max out his talent, but would not send him to a golf academy even if he could afford it. "I want Tyson to be well-rounded," he said. "Besides, I don't think I could send him to a boarding school. I'd miss him too much."

Mu Hu got a B on his steroids report. "I'll take it. My English teacher's psycho," he said. He flew to Shanghai to play in the European Tour's BMW Asian Open, shooting 73–74 to miss the cut by a single shot, but finishing eight strokes ahead of John Daly. His favorite day in China: driving indoor go-carts with his childhood friends at a huge Shanghai shopping mall.

Mu finished the year as the tenth-ranked junior boy in America. He turned eighteen on October 2. His birthday cake was orange and blue, the University of Florida's colors. He would join Bank Vongvanij in Gainesville in the fall of 2008, giving the Gators a Thai-Chi duo through 2011, unless one of them turns pro first. "I should be in Gainesville already," Mu said. "I'm dying to go, but my dad wants me to practice for another year." So Mu was spending a fifth year in high school, going to school for an hour a day. He practiced for seven hours a day, six days a week.

The Hus' home, a white-carpeted condo in a gated Del Webb development, was a two-minute drive from the ChampionsGate clubhouse. Visitors left their shoes at the door. Inside, Jenny Hu kept flowers in wide, filigreed Chinese vases, a reminder of home. All three family members were homesick. Jenny and Jian Song Hu planned to return to Shenzhen for good in 2008, when their son went off to college. Framed photos adorned the walls: Mu's swing sequence from *Golf*

Digest; Mu with his parents; Mu with Tiger Woods and Vijay Singh. One picture showed Mu with Leadbetter, who had signed it under the line *Mu, Keep chasing your dream.*

I asked Mu what his dream was. "Winning a major," he said. He wants to be the first Chinese golfer to win one. "And then I might go home."

Home to ChampionsGate?

"Home to China."

Mu slept in an orange and blue bedroom beside an end-table photo of Woods and Woods's agent, Mark Steinberg. Each morning he picked a neatly pressed, color-coordinated outfit from his closet. On his way to breakfast he passed his private workout area—blue mats, a physio ball, a wrist exerciser his father had fashioned from plastic piping, a wall mirror. Strips of masking tape on the mirror showed two swing-plane angles, one for the takeaway and one for the downswing—the same angles Leadbetter drew on his clunky video monitor twenty-five years before.

Mu nodded to Lead when they met on the range. It was a dignified gesture, a modified bow. They'd been working to keep Mu's head steady during the swing. After a few warm-ups, he laced a mid-iron into a light breeze. Watching it land, he said it had gone "179-ish." Ten minutes later he was belting majestic drives that carried one hundred yards farther.

"You'd better stop," Leadbetter said. "You can't hit one better than that."

Mu teed up another ball. "Oh, but I can."

In June 2007, **Gary Gilchrist** was replaced as director of the International Junior Golf Academy in Hilton Head, South

Carolina. The IJGA bumped him out and hired Hank Haney, Tiger Woods's swing coach. After losing Michelle Wie to Lead, Gilchrist had now been bigfooted by another famous-name teacher.

He turned his attention to a handful of LPGA and European pros who still listened to him. One of them, Norway's Suzann Pettersen, promptly won the LPGA Championship. A career underachiever who loved Gilchrist's rah-rah approach, Pettersen harnessed her immense talent, won four other tournaments and finished second to Lorena Ochoa on the LPGA money list. Her sudden stardom left her coach crowing.

"Am I jealous of David Leadbetter? No," Gilchrist told me. "But the question is, how much raw talent have we had to work with? David has had Charles Howell, Justin Rose, Aaron Baddeley, Michelle Wie, Ernie Els—some of the greatest talents of all time. I wish I'd had just one of those players!"

Always looking ahead, he was working on a training aid that would allow teens to get interactive golf instruction through their iPods. And now he was moving in on Lead's turf. Gilchrist, forty-four, was about to open a golf school at the Mission Inn Resort, just north of Orlando. He figured he couldn't get aced out of this one—the Gary Gilchrist International Golf Academy, opening in 2008.

Junior golf's premier sister act, **the Lendls**, went in different directions in the fall of 2007. Marika, the eldest, changed her college choice. Rather than go off to Vanderbilt, she switched to the University of Central Florida, where her coach would be Emilee Klein, a former LPGA pro. Ivan Lendl was pleased his daughter would be staying close to home. He still wasn't sure why someone planning a pro-sports career would want to spend four years sitting in classrooms, but mom Samantha understood. "Isabelle's all about golf," she said, "but Marika's more about life."

Isabelle, who looked like the next Annika Sorenstam as she rose to number three in the girls' rankings, turned sixteen in July. She lost ground in the fall, shooting a slew of 83s and 84s as her driver betrayed her. She was taking the club back too far inside, snap-hooking some drives and blocking others out-of-bounds to the right. Isabelle slid out of the top ten in the rankings while Ivan, sitting in his folding chair, watched for signs of folding in her. She earned his approval by soldiering on, keeping her head up as she studied the line of a bogey putt. "Losing can help if you learn from it," Ivan said. "I'm not concerned about how she does this week. I'm concerned about 2009."

In November, Isabelle won the World Golf Village Open. She followed that with an eventful Doherty Cup, a match play tournament in which she faced little sister Crash in the second round. Their father caddied for both players, back-breaking work for a creaky dad who would soon need a shot of novocaine in his spine. Crash led most of the day, only to watch Isabelle sink three putts of fifty-plus feet to beat her.

The victor consoled her tearful sis on the way home. "Crash, you played great," she said.

Crash didn't want to hear it. "Yeah, thanks, but you suck!"

Ivan said the post-match ride was important for both girls. "Isabelle did the right thing, praising her sister with honesty. Crash was too upset to listen, but she'd remember it later."

In the semifinals, a nervous Isabelle edged big sister Marika. That put her in the Doherty Cup final against twenty-nine-year-old amateur star Meghan Bolger, the women's golf coach at the University of Mississippi. Isabelle scouted Bolger the modern way: "I Googled her." Then beat her to win the tournament, with Dad lugging the bag.

Michelle Wie was still seeking a breakthrough that would prove she belonged at the game's highest level. In August, the six-foot-one Hawaiian became the most conspicuous Stanford freshman since Chelsea Clinton a decade before. In October, soon after taking her first college classes, including courses in Japanese and hip-hop dancing, Michelle turned eighteen. But she wasn't on campus for her birthday. She was in Palm Desert, California, playing in the LPGA's Samsung World Championship on a sponsor's exemption. After two rounds of 79 she was twenty-three strokes off the lead. Walking with her head down, she finished nineteenth in a 20-player field, thirty-six shots behind former AJGA star Lorena Ochoa. Still winless in two years as a pro, Michelle finished the year with on-course earnings of $23,024 and off-course earnings of about $20 million. Her endorsement income was sure to drop in 2008.

The day after the Samsung, her manager, Greg Nared, resigned. Nared had made his managerial bones in eight action-packed years with Tiger Woods, but a year with Team Wie had been too much for him.

Michelle returned to ChampionsGate to work with Lead-better. It had pained him to see her playing hurt. "There was no reason for her to go through that," he said. "She was flinching at impact. She'd lost the big coil and lag that gave her power." He restored some of her power with a new drill: Lead knelt on the range, flipping tennis balls that Michelle clouted with a baseball bat. *Bang!* A powder-puff hitter at first, she was soon bopping liners past the 100-yard marker.

At her next pro event, the LPGA's Fields Open in Hawaii, she hit several booming drives including one that went 320 yards. She made the cut, but faded to a last-place tie, and crit-ics blasted her. Some blamed "Lead poisoning" as well as pa-rental interference. "She has become overwhelmed with mechanics," wrote *Sports Illustrated Golf Plus* columnist Dot-tie Pepper, "getting input from not only teacher David Lead-better but also her dad, B.J. The big, flowing, athletic swing Michelle had as a thirteen-, fourteen-, and fifteen-year-old world-beater is sadly a thing of the past."

That line irked Leadbetter. "Yes, her swing used to be long and fluid and beautiful," he said. "She was a thin, thirteen-year-old girl, for crying out loud! Now she's eighteen. A woman. Bigger, stronger, filled out. It's ridiculous to expect her to swing like she did at thirteen. For me, the question is, Is she playing enough golf? It's tough to compete with full-time golf-ers if you're worrying about an English exam. Practicing two hours a day, going to college—can she keep up with Lorena and Annika?"

Michelle was upbeat. She loved life at Stanford, where parents are not allowed to stay overnight in the dorms. Still, there was reason to think that the choices she and her parents made in 2007 may have changed the future of women's golf.

"My wrist feels better, except for the fact that it's never going to be 100 percent ever again," she said. "It's never going to be like it was before."

David Leadbetter turned fifty-five in June 2007. Each day he slathered sunblock on every inch of exposed, mottled skin. By the end of the year, Michelle Wie's troubles had added a gray strand or two to his hairline. He appointed a new caddie for her: Tim Vickers, a Leadbetter instructor based at ChampionsGate. Michelle and her parents announced that she would skip the 2008 spring quarter at Stanford to work on her golf game, and Leadbetter hinted that she might still learn to say no to her father. "She needs to have a say in her own career," he said.

While juggling his duties to Michelle, Trevor Immelman, Charles Howell III and more than a dozen other pros, Lead was also working to resurrect Ernie Els's career. At thirty-seven, the Big Easy wasn't finding the game so easy anymore. Leadbetter, who had coached Els for seventeen years, had never known such a natural golfer. The easygoing South African could take a month off to drink beer and lounge around his house—a brick mansion with an African-style thatched roof at England's Wentworth Club, near Windsor Castle— and then catch a plane and win a Tour event. But a knee injury had ruined what Leadbetter called Ernie's "beautiful rhythm." As the year dragged on, Els favored his left knee. He tried to compensate with extra hand and wrist action, and sprayed the ball at unexpected angles. His confidence wavered. "Ernie hit some wild shots he had never hit before, and it scared him." Els was already in a shaky place mentally. He and Lead had often discussed his dilemma: Els may have been the only golfer with the raw physical talent to compete with Tiger Woods, but he lacked Woods's fierce ambition, and he knew it. "We talked about Tiger," Lead said, "and how hard it is to have somebody like Tiger in your generation."

With Leadbetter's help, Els grooved his post-injury swing. He won the 2008 Honda Classic, his first Tour victory in three years.

Three weeks later, Els left Leadbetter to work with Lead's rival Butch Harmon. So goes the dance of swing coaches and elite golfers. Leadbetter kept his bony chin up. He shrugged and turned to his other students, including the powerful, precocious Finau brothers of Salt Lake City, Tony and Gipper. Both turned pro in 2007, the year Tony turned eighteen and Gipper turned seventeen. Both Finau brothers generated clubhead speeds of 135 miles per hour, about 10 miles per hour more than Tiger Woods, and ball speeds topping 200. They routinely clouted 350-yard drives, with occasional pokes of 400-plus. At the PGA Tour's 2007 U.S. Bank Championship, Tony drove his ball on or over the green on seven par-four holes.

And finally, three weeks after Els dumped him, Leadbetter got the sweetest possible payback: His star student Trevor Immelman won the Masters.

By then, Bradenton had been buzzing for months with news of a new arrival. While other students began the 2007–2008 school year with hugs and fist bumps in the Leadbetter Academy parking lot, fifteen-year-old Oscar Sharpe practiced alone at the end of the range. Oscar was England's best-known junior golfer since Faldo. The English press called him "Britain's answer to Tiger Woods." Short and spindly, with jet-black hair cut sharp as a pop star's, Oscar was about to give Peter Uihlein a rival as the Bradenton Bunch's top banana.

He was homesick at first. Oscar missed his parents, who had gone home to Cheltenham after his first two days at the Academy. He admitted he was "wishing for a hug from Mum and Dad." He muddled through by "distracting meself" with strict routine: up at 5:30 a.m. for a run, followed by two hours on the range, breakfast, classes at Pendleton, a quick lunch, four more hours on the range and a two-hour workout in the gym. Unlike most range rats, Oscar focused mostly on his short game. He would circle a practice green from sixty yards out, attacking the pin with high floaters, humpbacked bloops and low bullets, sometimes stepping on a ball to worsen his lie. After an hour he moved to a different green for putting practice, which began with a hundred four-footers, a hundred ten-footers, and a hundred "easy ones" of three feet.

In his first meeting with Leadbetter, the guru impressed him with a quick fix. He straightened Oscar's left arm. Moments later the boy was smacking long, pure draws and power fades, working the ball like the shot-shapers of old—and doing it with cool poise that left the teacher shaking his head. "I felt like *I* was auditioning for *him*," says Leadbetter.

Oscar won the first two US junior tournaments he entered. One evening in early 2008 he was practicing alone, rolling his hundred ten-footers on the Academy's artificial-turf green. He preferred the artificial green because it was slicker than grass greens. "More challenging," he said.

He knew he wasn't the first "next Tiger" and probably

wouldn't be the last. He knew how hungry golf writers were for the next-Tiger-of-the-month, but the hype didn't faze him because Oscar Sharpe knew who and what he was—a gifted, driven boy with miles and miles to go before he teed it up with Tiger, but with the right idea: "All I want is to get the absolute most out of meself," he said. "Beginning with this next putt."

He started it rolling.

In October, seven hundred miles north of the Leadbetter Academy, more than one hundred worshippers filled the Beaver Creek Church of the Brethren in the one-stoplight county of Floyd, Virginia. **Michael Wade** couldn't make it. He was practicing with his high school team, and anyway he would have been embarrassed to be in church that morning, because his dad was preaching about him.

Pastor Marvin Wade started with the week's announcements: choir practice, an upcoming hayride, a chili cook-off. The pastor stood before a gold-plated cross, flanked by candles, a lazy ceiling fan turning overhead. He wore a white pullover that clung to his ample stomach, with a little microphone clipped to his pocket.

"Our scripture is Galatians, chapter four, verses one to seven, on the adoption of sons," he said. "My message this morning: Hallelujah Adoption."

Marvin paced as he preached. After reading the Bible passage, he told the congregation that he'd grown up without a dad. His father had died in a car wreck when Marvin was a year old. Many years later he and his wife, Sandy, "tried and tried to have children, but we couldn't, and that made a great big void in our lives." They tried adopting, but there was a long wait and the cost of up to $15,000 was beyond their means. "I came into this church," he said, his voice rising, "and I got down on my knees and cried out to God for a child of my own!"

Now Marvin was in what he called his preachin' gear, with goose bumps he called Holy Ghost bumps on his arms.

He and Sandy heard about an agency in West Salem that helped parents adopt at-risk kids who had been in foster care. After ten weeks of classes and filling out forms, they met with a social worker and a troubled eight-year-old boy at a nearby Pizza Inn. "I told the Lord I'd know my son when I saw him. And I did. The moment I laid eyes on that little boy," Pastor Wade said, "I knew." Next came a struggle with four state and local agencies to work out the adoption. At last came the phone call he and Sandy had prayed for: *Come and get him.*

"Hallelujah!" he shouted, his voice filling his little brick church. Other voices answered: *Hallelujah! Praise God!* Marvin Wade mopped his brow with a handkerchief. "And what we done to get Michael, well, it does not compare to what God did to get you."

He told about the day he and Sandy signed Michael's adoption papers. "Signed in ink," he said. "But you know what? *God* wants to adopt *you*, and those adoption papers are signed in the blood of Jesus. God invites you to be part of his family. He wants a close relationship. He wants us to turn to him and say, 'You're my dad.'"

The church was quiet. Marvin took a sip of water before adding a personal note: As everyone here today knew, he said,

Michael had a great talent at golf. Marvin believed that Michael's golf talent might not be for Michael's benefit alone. Not if he kept getting better, not if people heard about his golf and wanted to know his life story. "Someday, someone might come to know Jesus because of Michael Wade from Floyd, Virginia."

Outside, the leaves were starting to turn. The crests of the Blue Ridge Mountains rose into mist. Marvin and Michael spent the afternoon playing a friendly round at Botetourt Country Club in Troutville.

Portly Marvin took a Dalyesque rip at the ball. He tried needling his son to throw him off: "That's a slick putt, Michael. It'll roll down yonder way." But it didn't work. Seventeen-year-old Michael, sporting a thin mustache and goatee he hoped made him look older, sank the putt. On the next hole he whammed a drive over a 70-foot pine that was 220 yards from the tee. His violent, shouldery swing sent his cap flying. The cap fell behind him. The ball rose, carrying a yard or two over the top of the tree.

Michael had decided to play college golf for Radford University, twenty miles from home. He would be able to see his girlfriend, Mandy, every weekend. He said he was going to marry her. "Don't tell my dad yet. He thinks we're awful young." Michael had been working construction for Mandy's father, a contractor, and planned to "build our house with my own hands."

Deer watched from the woods behind the next green. Michael talked about how he'd bagged a ten-point buck with his light little .243 rifle the year before. He had always been good at anything that took eye-hand coordination. He remembered his earliest golf practice, after Marvin introduced him to the game. They lived in Bassett, Virginia, back then, and Marvin's church adjoined a playground. Twelve-year-old Michael spent hours hitting pitch shots over a ditch toward a swing set fifty yards away, aiming for the swings. A year later, in one of his first full rounds at Great Oaks Country Club, he shot 67.

He wanted to play on the PGA Tour. "That's a long way from here," he said, "but it's doable." And if he never made the Tour? "Well, there's the Nationwide Tour. And if not that, maybe I'll be a club pro someplace. That's a pretty good job."

The 15th hole was a short par-four, 281 yards dead uphill, the green protected by pines. "Driveable for you," Marvin said. True enough—Michael once hit a ball 361 yards in a long-drive contest. But this was a bad bet. Only a perfect drive would clear the trees and reach the green.

"I'm goin' for it."

He swung, hat flying. "Hoo-ee, that's *way* right," Marvin said.

Michael spat on the ground. His drive was out-of-bounds. Lying two on the tee, he teed up another ball and swung just as hard. This drive was better. In fact, when we reached the green we found his ball five feet from the hole. He knocked it in for a par.

As we played the next hole, he said he often thought about his earlier life. His birth mother was "still out there," he said. "Last I heard she was living behind Wal-Mart." But it wasn't his mother who haunted him. It was his little sister, Ginny, who was four years old when eight-year-old Michael was adopted by the Wades and escaped the foster-care system. He remembered one of the last things his mother had said to him before the state took her children away. "Watch out for your sister," she said. "Take care of her."

Nine years later, Michael shivered. "I always blame myself," he said, "because my sister is still in that system I got out of. She may still be getting beat up every night."

We were running out of sun. There wouldn't be time to finish the round. "One more hole," Marvin said.

Our last hole was an uphill par-three, 174 to the flag. I hit a five-iron. Michael hit a towering eight-iron. The ball hung in the darkening sky, heading straight for the flag.

"That's a peach!" Pastor Marvin said. "That one might just be in."

ACKNOWLEDGMENTS

Driven would have dribbled off the tee without David Leadbetter's help. He was generous with his time, candid in his
comments and eager to help my readers understand his work,
all while knowing he would have no say in what I wrote. I
admire him.

Lead's lieutenants Blaik Shew and Darin Tennyson were
crucial, too. Both had their plates overfull before adding my
needs to their duties for a year and a half. Blaik showed me
around Leadbetter headquarters in ChampionsGate, Florida,
and always pointed me in the right direction. Darin, who became my go-to guy at ChampionsGate, was sharp, upbeat
and efficient at every turn. Both men remind me of world-
class golfers: They make a hard job look easy.

At the Leadbetter Academy in Bradenton, David Whelan
welcomed me, and Tracy Reiser made every visit a breeze. If
not for Tracy, I would still be sitting outside the security gate
on 34th Street West, drumming my fingers on the wheel of

my rental car. After a few weeks on the job I became a fan of Academy instructor Tim Sheredy, whose enthusiasm for his players is infectious. Golf magazine editors looking for the next star teacher should sign Sheredy up now. Thanks also to Malcolm Joseph, Mark Rummings, Andrew Park, Andrew Oliphant, Shane Reiser, Bobby Verwey, Phil Parkin and former Lead lieutenant Steve Wakulsky. I am also grateful to IMG vice president Ted Meekma, a tennis guy who knows a great deal about golf; the inimitable Nick Bollettieri; Steve Shenbaum and Blair Dalton of Game On and mental conditioner Chris Passarella.

Many thanks to the parents who invited me into their families' lives, particularly Ivan Lendl, one of five unforgettable Lendls I met; the Wades of Floyd, Virginia; the Hu family of China and Florida and the Winegardners of Maryland. Tina Uihlein, John Francis, Wallace and Pauline Booth and Bora Park contributed as well.

Gary Gilchrist provided several of the most interesting golf conversations I have ever had. Ditto for Mike Bender, Dr. Jim Loehr and Dr. Tim Sell of the University of Pittsburgh Medical Center. David Feherty, Nick Price, Nick Faldo, Brandel Chamblee, Mitchell Spearman, Gary Van Sickle, Rich O'Dell and Rick Lipsey contributed key details.

On the publishing side, I was lucky to be paired with Bill Shinker, a great friend of golf and of his writers; and literary agent Scott Waxman. Editor Patrick Mulligan completed the foursome. His work improved the book. Farley Chase and Melissa Sarver of the Waxman Agency improved my year, as usual.

On the home front, I am endlessly grateful to the loves of

my life: Lily, Cal and my in-house editor, Pamela. Thanks for putting up with my road trips and greeting me with open arms when I come home.

Most of all, thanks to the young golfers who are the heroes and heroines of this book.